CAHIERS DU CINEMA PRESENTS

THE HOLLYWOOD INTERVIEWS

D1565920

TALKING IMAGES SERIES

edited by Yann Perreau

Series ISSN 1744–9901

Previously published in this series:

Cinema: The Archaeology of Film & the Memory of a Century
Jean-Luc Godard & Youssef Ishaghpour

Film Fables   Jacques Rancière

Visions of England: Class & Culture in Contemporary Cinema
Paul Dave

Forthcoming

Film World: The Directors' Interviews   Michel Ciment

CAHIERS DU CINEMA PRESENTS

THE HOLLYWOOD INTERVIEWS

Oxford • New York

This work is published with the support of the French Ministry of Culture –
Centre National du Livre

Liberté • Égalité • Fraternité
RÉPUBLIQUE FRANÇAISE

This book is supported by the French Ministry for Foreign Affairs as part of the
Burgess Programme headed for the French Embassy in London by the Institut
Français du Royaume-Uni

First published in France, 1995, by Cahiers du Cinéma
© Cahiers du Cinéma, 1995, *15 ans de cinéma américain*

This English translation by John Flowers © Berg Publishers 2006

Paperback edition reprinted 2006

Photographs copyright Cahiers du Cinéma

English edition
First published in 2006 by
Berg
Editorial offices:
First Floor, Angel Court, 81 St Clements Street, Oxford OX4 1AW, UK
175 Fifth Avenue, New York, NY 10010, USA

Berg is the imprint of Oxford International Publishers Ltd.

Library of Congress Cataloging-in-Publication Data
A catalogue record for this book is available from the Library of Congress.

British Library Cataloguing-in-Publication Data
A catalogue record for this book is available from the British Library.

ISBN-13 978 1 84520 440 2 (Cloth)
         978 1 84520 441 9 (Paper)

ISBN-10 1 84520 440 9 (Cloth)
         1 84520 441 7 (Paper)

Typeset by JS Typesetting Ltd, Porthcawl, Mid Glamorgan
Printed in the United States.

www.bergpublishers.com

Contents

The Challenge to Hollywood: The Arrival of
the *Auteur*   1

Part I The Interviews

1   Martin Scorsese   9
2   Clint Eastwood   41
3   Francis Ford Coppola   61
4   Brian De Palma   83
5   Joel and Ethan Coen   101
6   Tim Burton   121

Filmographies   147

Acknowledgments   153

The Challenge to Hollywood: The Arrival of the Auteur

The history of Hollywood across the years is made up of a series of changes and mishaps that have radically changed the relationship between film-makers and the film industry. As is well known, Hollywood's life goes in cycles during which the industrial machine that it has become pulls in and then rejects its *auteurs* at its discretion. Such is Hollywood. It is capricious and suffers from periods of manic depression, and the best directors have to turn to subterfuge when the studios, without any warning, turn cold.

The idea of the *auteur* may have been brought in under cover by American filmmakers in the 1950s, but those who came after them shouted loud and clear about their right to have total control over their films, an idea that was not common at the time when they entered the Hollywood scene. Hollywood found it difficult to take on board the idea that a film was not a collective venture, something conceived by a group made up of a director, actors, producer and scriptwriters. In the 1960s and 1970s, however, there was a marked change in thinking thanks to the arrival of a new generation of independent directors who came from television and the universities.

We can say with certainty that Hollywood finally accepted the idea of the *auteur* in the 1970s. Whether, like Martin Scorsese, Michael Cimino and Terrence Malick, the best directors worked within the system or, like John Cassavetes, on its boundaries, they succeeded in imposing the idea of the director as the *auteur* of a film. This generation, which grew out of the schools of film studies, was the first to have been shaped by a love of the cinema that was transmitted through institutions like the universities. These filmmakers came to know the Hollywood cinema through the east-coast critical reception of European cinema.

But this would change again. In the early years of the 1980s films like *Blow Out* (1981), *Raging Bull* (1980), *Apocalypse Now* (1979) or *Heaven's Gate* (1980) heralded the end of an era, that of the "super *auteur* films" conceived and made with the resources of the film industry. The studios changed direction and this generation was now marginalized. They preferred to have craftsmen, scriptwriters and actors who could be more easily controlled than those directors who were considered by the executives of the major studios to be too expensive and capricious. Only two *auteur*-actors, Woody Allen and Clint Eastwood, would be able to maintain their independence; the first because he worked on the edge of Hollywood, the second because in his own way he was already part of the star system.

In the 1980s the cinema as spectacle became a winner. The development of special effects and new technology went hand in hand with a new aesthetic derived from advertising and publicity. Hollywood preferred to turn again – and with success – towards well-established formulae and genre films. Studios put their faith in experienced directors, and the *auteur* tradition that had developed in the 1960s suffered. Having been pampered previously, the directors who had appeared on the scene in the previous decade now had to prove that they were just as good at making films as the hack workers employed by the studios. The wager would be won by Scorsese, Coppola, Cimino and De Palma, who were better directors than most of those whose films were successful, and by the 1990s there would be yet another change in Hollywood's thinking. With studio directors and stars, who were becoming

3

increasingly capricious and making a number of blunders and with the serious failure of several studio productions the economic good sense of the 1980s was called into question. This was a period when the major directors were on ejector seats. There was then a search for new blood and, curiously, those nonconformist directors who had previously been marginalized were to make their come back. In this context "veterans" like Scorsese, Coppola and Eastwood were commercially successful and benefited from critical recognition. They also gave support to some of the younger filmmakers, providing them with contacts with the studios, while others, like Tim Burton and Ethan and Joel Coen, had the intelligence to adapt genre films, all the time asserting their individuality.

Since the mid 1990s something important has occurred in US cinema. Things have moved forward in a remarkable way and failure is not forgiven. If the Hollywood of today doesn't hesitate to promote its young talent, it is equally ready to get rid of them. The change from the rejection of the *auteurs* to their return in strength constitutes one of the natural cycles within the history of cinema of the USA.

The relationship these *auteurs* have with the Hollywood industry is complex. Because they have accepted it as the vehicle for their talents within it certain directors have sometimes had to make concessions, to compromise and find ways of dealing with those responsible for funding. Scorsese, Coppola and Tim Burton give their own accounts of their struggle as Californian filmmakers The younger ones have to avoid being mashed up by the machine while knowing how to take their chance. Others again have to forget their *auteur* super-ego in order to make a film that at least in appearance is more impersonal.

The relationship between the filmmaker and the idea of the *auteur* is fundamental to the history of US cinema. Whenever their position is in danger the principal *auteurs* have always shown that they can be first-rate filmmakers, and it is no doubt because they are the best that in the end they always win.

The interviews in this book are full of rich insights into the position of the *auteur* caught between the rigors of an economic system driven by demand and the desire to express himself personally, they also reflect the constant to-ing and fro-ing between the film industry and its most talented filmmakers.

Acknowledgments

The interviews in this book were conducted for *Cahiers du Cinéma* at different times and in different places. Details on each one can be found at the end of the book.

Part I
The Interviews

Martin Scorsese

Why did you decide to make a film of Goodfellas*?*

Martin Scorsese: Because of the book. I liked it.

Have you changed any parts of it?

MS: No, it's a straightforward, simple adaptation. The main problem was how to choose the scenes we wanted to keep and those we wanted to discard. I didn't want any story, any plot. That was easier for me. That was one of the reasons why we decided not to use two marvelous passages in the book – the Air France hold up and the Lufthansa business. What's more, my generation is one, when we were children, that saw *Durififi chez les hommes* [Jules Dassin, 1955] and *The Asphalt Jungle* [John Huston, 1950]. I saw these films when I was ten and I said to myself that it wasn't worth trying to do that again. They're not marvelous films, you could make them again today, but I wasn't interested. What I was really interested in was the day-to-day life of a criminal "clan" but not from the point of view of their leaders. For years we've had fascinating films about the rise and fall of great men. In the case of gangsters you can't really talk about greatness unless it's in the way that greatness can be perverted. But as the years have gone by people have become increasingly drawn to this kind of story because of films like *The Public Enemy* [William Wellman, 1931] and *Scarface* [Howard Hawks, 1932]. *The Public Enemy* is very important to me; I saw it when I was eight or ten, but I only saw *Scarface*, which I love, when I was making *Taxi Driver* in 1976. Howard Hughes had blocked the rights and it was impossible to see it in the States. For several years you could see it in France or England, but I never saw it. It's a film that has become very important for me.

I didn't want to make a film about organized crime, but I didn't want to make one that showed the rise and fall of an individual and even less about an individual whose power was assured. I wanted to describe how criminals lived and that's the only reason that made me shoot *Goodfellas*. As you can see in the films produced by Warner you have classic stories all from the same time, and with *The Godfather* the account of the rise and fall of an individual came to an end and we had that of a whole family. *The Godfather: Part III* comes out this year. There was no reason why I should make a film

10

about Bugsy Siegel or Legs Diamond ... all these stories are fantastic. But at this stage of my career now there's absolutely no reason for me to tackle this kind of day-to-day story – how these people dress, what they eat (eating is a very important ritual). And this kind of quiet violence as well. For example, at the end of the film when Jimmy and Henry meet in the diner the camera focuses on Jimmy and then on Henry and you hear his voice that says: "That's it, he's going to kill me," and Jimmy gives his order to the waitress: "We'll have muffins." That's all he says. I much prefer this kind of tension to the traditional endings with their explosions and car chases.

The film is like a documentary.

MS: Precisely. I haven't looked for any pretexts, by which I mean that I've used the voice off to tell the story right to the end. And that's why I've allowed myself to stop the film from time to time to explain something or other to the public. The dramatic moments of the film are less important than the way it unfolds and allows the spectator to become immersed in the life of the characters. It didn't matter at all to me to stop the action from time to time and allow the character to speak directly to the camera. That's what happens at the end.

The series of shots gives the impression that the film is moving faster than the voice off...

11

MS: After a while the voice off has no other significance than to indicate certain things precisely, like "The body of ... was found there" or "Jimmy did this" "Jimmy did that." For example, in the helicopter sequence when Henry is under the influence of cocaine, you're absolutely right; the voice off is completely detached and that's something I wanted to show as well. I wanted the audience to experience the physical and emotional state of someone who has been taking cocaine for three years – coke or amphetamines. Something that means you becomes so excited that you lose all control over how things are perceived and how you drift into a kind of paranoia. When you have this kind of life and are addicted to this extent, it becomes impossible to function normally. Everything assumes the same importance – the invalid chair, the helicopter, tomato sauce, weapons, drugs, Jimmy, his wife... If one of them had still been fully aware, they would have noticed this bitch of a helicopter, they would have spotted it during the previous weeks and realized that they shouldn't go out on that day. But no, and all because of drugs and this kind of life. That's what I wanted the audience – who have never taken this kind of drug or who have never been involved in this kind of life – to feel. I wanted to give the impression of the kind of anguish, paranoia and panic that comes from this way of living. That's why, after a while, and above all just after he avoids an accident, the voice off simply becomes a non-stop babble in his head: "I must do that, and after that, and after that bla bla bla." What he's saying no longer means anything. What's most important is his mental state. And that's the trick, because throughout the film the audience tries to follow what the voice off is saying. But in this sequence the voice off is out of control. Everything is out of control. His life is out of control. And then when a gun is put to his head it's almost a relief to him. The audience feels that like a sigh of relief. The character says "Take me away, throw me into prison, kill me, do what you want to me. I can't go on, I can't go on like this any more." That's the principal idea. Just making films makes me have days like that, so add to that drugs and a criminal life style... It's something absolutely fascinating that I've always wanted to show, and this film gave me the ideal opportunity to try.

You have the impression that the voice off protects the viewer from the film's violence.

MS: That's for you to tell me.

Still, the film is very violent. For example, the scene when Harry breaks his neighbor's nose...

13

MS: But there's only a general shot, no close up. It begins with him getting out of the car, then he hits the guy in the face and leaves. It's simple.

The scene in which Joe Pesci kills the young man is horrible.

MS: That's true. That scene, the death of the young man, is dreadful. And yet when he kills him it's not so violent as all that. I think we are talking about the difference between your idea of violence and mine. When Spider guns the boy down we don't see much blood. What's awful is the action itself. That goes much deeper. To see a body blown into a thousand pieces is different. Perhaps we need to talk to a psychologist or a psychiatrist or a sociologist. I wonder why it is that nowadays we see more and more special effects showing mutilated or decomposing bodies. It's as though there is a growing need for this kind of thing. At the same time, all that goes back to the Punch and Judy tradition that dates from the nineteenth century, I think, and even before that there were public executions.[1] Perhaps it's linked with the theater. But what's more disturbing in the film is probably Spider's attitude. In that scene there's not much bloodshed; what shocks is the way it all develops, just like that, at a click of the fingers.

Almost indifferently.

MS: Yes ... the other had told him to fuck off, and that's his reply. It's pure madness. [*Silence*] As for the neighbor, he get's beaten up because he threw the girl out of the car. At least, that's what we can suppose. It's what she tells Henry. We don't see him. In this world, violence is the main way people express themselves ... in fact if we're honest about it, in the whole world. We're supposed to be civilized, but, after all, the reactions here when my film *The Last Temptation of Christ* came out were the worst in the world. It really surprised me. It's fascinating. Amazing. You could go on talking about it... And yet we always come back to that. All it needs is for someone to hit someone else and the discussion stops. It's madness. I grew up with that, you know. I was in a church and was beginning to take a serious interest in religion, in Jesus, in loving one's neighbor, in forgiveness ... and then when I came out of the church I would see a gangster beating up somebody or kids hitting Puerto Ricans because they didn't want them in their district. People were worried that they would bring down the whole Italian–American social structure and the answer to the problem was to beat them up, to kill them. It's completely depressing.

At the end of the film Henry is at rock bottom: there's nothing left, no more forgiveness, nothing at all...

MS: What's fantastic at the end of the book is that he doesn't say "I'm sorry for what I've done" because the story doesn't stop there – Henry Hill is still alive and is responsible for quite a lot of fishy goings on. What's interesting is that he is neither a smart talker nor a hypocrite and that he doesn't say "I'm sorry, I really am sorry for what I've done and I'd like to say to the kids who see me not to make the same mistakes as me, not to become gangsters." What he says is: "I'm sorry I can't lead that sort of life any more." That's very straightforward and honest of him. I wasn't thinking about children when I made the film [*Laughter.*] even if I think they should see it. There are children of a certain age who can let themselves be seduced and dragged along by the brilliance and the danger of a life of crime. And they let themselves get sucked in, like Henry, and then Spider is dead and then Billy Basket, and then his wife takes against him and his whole life gradually falls apart. From that point on it would be easy to create an outdated moral tale. I don't think that there is no more hope or possibility of redemption. There's always a glimmer of hope... It all depends on what you believe in. In Henry's case he was happy to be a "wise guy" all the same. He got arrested for drug trafficking and being drunk.

But there's no more "family"...

MS: Look what he did! The life he led! These guys don't care about anything, about you, me, films, God... They couldn't care less about anything.

It could be said that Goodfellas *is both a follow up to* Mean Streets *and its opposite.*

MS: Yes, it's completely its opposite. The characters in *Mean Streets* are not on the same level as Henry, and Henry is way down below Paul Sorvino or James Conway on the social ladder. The characters in *Mean Streets* are really Italian–American kids who are mixed up in this society. I'm the inspiration for the character of Charlie. In some scenes we even see him at university, at NYU. I used to live on the east side of Manhattan, the Lower East side. There's Houston Street, and if you go west six or seven blocks up from Houston you reach Greenwich Village and there you have NYU and the other big Italian–American district. The two "little Italys." The Italian community to the west is a lot more tolerant and more open to other cultures. There's Greenwich Village where you can find everything – artists, poets, painters, homosexuals, dancers... The difference is like the one that separates the Left Bank from the Right. There's something like a "Left-Bank" culture. And you have to imagine then an Italian community in the middle of the Left Bank. They're more receptive of other cultures. And in addition there's NYU, which is symbolic. It goes back to the nineteenth century and is the oldest university in the States. By American standards that's pretty old. On the East side, where I lived, there was nothing like that. There were only Italian–Americans and inside that community Sicilians, Calabrians and Neapolitans making up very distinct groups. In *Mean Streets* my character is always going from the East to the West Side. I had written the scenes in which you watched him taking courses at the university. At the time I lived on Elizabeth Street. There was nowhere to go. Nothing changed. During this period of my life I had friends, half of whose lives were spent in the "wise guy" culture and who didn't want to have anything to do with those types. The character in *Goodfellas* only wants one thing – and that's to become a "wise guy." It's the only thing he's worried about.

Why did you begin this film with the scene that we see later, in the middle?

MS: The reason's simple: I wanted to avoid having the film start with the image of a boy watching gangsters through his window. That's really boring. After that I'd have followed up with his rise and fall. So by starting the film with this sequence I could convey the essence of this kind of criminal life. If you're going to become a "wise guy" you have to kill and have the balls to do it. If you don't, then you might as well not bother. That's why I began the film with the murder scene. I took the middle of the film and put it at the start, that's all.

You feel that the character is already condemned, that his fate is already marked out...

MS: That's true, but at the same time there's something a bit striking about it. He says "All my life I've wanted to be a gangster." And this is what that means. You have to know what to do with a corpse. Sometimes you bury it, sometimes you cut it up into pieces. Four months ago a group of Italian "wise guys" were arrested. They were paid killers, experts who got rid of bodies by chopping them up and burying them later on Staten Island. The pieces were found. It was the work of specialists. You have to know how to do it properly.

All your characters are obsessed, they're psychopaths. And their energy comes from their obsession.

MS: Yes, it seems so. I'll never be interested in a character who can't make up his mind, who'll do one thing one day and another the day after, who can't come to a decision. I find that boring and un-dramatic. I'm attracted to people who are obstinate

19

and pig-headed. Once you're with characters like that you know nothing can stop them and that they are more or less "bound to succeed."

You always have the impression with your films that there is no screen between the film and the act of watching. The audience is in the film. That's very different from De Palma's films when you feel the audience is being impelled towards the film. You don't play on that except in the scene between de Niro and Henry's wife, under the bridge. That scene is right out of Hitchcock.

MS: I wanted to use all possible styles. By that I mean all the different film idioms possible from Griffith to Hitchcock. One particular style wasn't important for me. I wanted to use different ways of telling a story with images that would provoke different emotions, even different psychological reactions. In the shot when she goes down into the street to see whether there are any clothes, it's done as in a thriller. The camera follows what the woman sees. We see Bob de Niro pointing with his finger, telling her from inside to go in, but in such a way that we don't really know whether she is in danger. Nor, to this day, does Karen know. She never knew whether Jimmy sent her there to get killed, kidnapped or anything else. And I found it interesting to put the audience in this state of mind, especially at this point in the film. Karen says to her husband, "Why don't you stay in prison?" and he replies, "If I don't get out they'll kill me." She thinks he's paranoid and suddenly she becomes aware of the risks, she feels something strange about Jimmy, "Uncle Jimmy," who's almost a member of the family, almost a father to her, and she says to herself, yes, something could happen… Even now she still doesn't know what it is, but I wanted the audience to have the same feeling: she starts to feel something for the first time. Her life could be in danger from those close to her. That's also something I underlined in the film. The characters never mix with people outside, they are always together. When I made the film I did it as though I was the audience and I want to be entertained; it's a very self-centered way of going about things. I don't know whether it's good, but it's like that when I'm working. Brian De Palma, who is one of my best friends, works in a completely opposite way. He's always thinking about the public. Me, I don't, because I am the public. That's how I see things. I see lots of different films but the ones I watch again most often – because of their formal construction, their direction and the way they are edited – are those by Hitchcock and, of course, those by Powell and Pressburger. Of course, I've got some reservations about Hitchcock: the way the actors perform and the stories, but I really like the way the films are edited and shot. Take *The Birds* [1963], for example. I love the first hour of the film. The second is tremendous but I love the first because of the quality of the shots: the movement or lack of movement in the frame, the way the characters move or the cameras are used – tracking shots, panoramas, wide shots or shortened ones. For me it's like music. I watch these films a lot: *Vertigo* [1958], *The Birds*, *The Man who Knew Too Much* [1956], in particular the color films of the 1950s – *Rear Window* [1954], up to a certain point. I prefer the others for the way they are directed. But that has nothing to do with what I do. Still, I do make use of them. I do the same with films by Powell and Pressburger – they're more romantic and emotional. In particular *The Red Shoes* [1948] and *Colonel Blimp* [1943]. Michael Powell and I have become close friends and he married my editor, Thelma Schoonmaker. I often watch his films. Sometimes at home I let them run on 16 mm or on video while I do something else. It's like moving painting. I don't know what the best way is. It's always the same story, the one Hitchcock used to tell about *Sabotage* [1936]. Should you set the bomb up and tell the audience in such a way they are captured by the suspense during the conversation that takes place between the characters? Or should you choose another way that would be not to say anything at all? The characters are talking and suddenly there is an explosion. Which is better? Is one really better than the other? For me life is like the second. But perhaps Hitchcock wasn't interested in reproducing life in the cinema; he was interested in something else. What I mean by that is that he didn't set out to reproduce life as he saw it. Life, for me, is a shock, full of surprises and has that mad element that means that you don't know what's going to happen from one minute to the next. There's no "reality," just something that exists now and then disappears before you have time to become aware of it. [*Laughter.*]

Karen accepts men's laws. Do you think that one say you will create a female character who will behave in a way that is not dictated by men?

MS: Yes. [*Silence.*] In this kind of society women don't see the violence at all. That's why, at the end, Karen thinks Jimmy is trying to have her killed, though she's not sure. No one really knows. And then she begins to understand what this violence is like. There's the scene of the fight in the bar, with Joe Pesci. There's a young girl there but we don't see her again afterwards. I'm talking about a world in which, in general, men are against men. To be faithful to the world I'm depicting I give women secondary roles. It's like that. Even in *New York Stories*, the artist is a man. That doesn't mean that the young girl will not be a great artist. But she's twenty-one and beginning. I wasn't interested in who had the dominant part in the relationship. What interested me was the teacher–pupil relationship in one that was also amorous. But I'm planning two films in which a woman will have an important part.

As in Alice Doesn't Live Here Anymore?

MS: No, not really. I'm planning a period piece in which the women will have a central part, a life to lead and a way of organizing things, while the men will be more or less slaves to convention.[2]

Why do we have the exchange between the hero and the woman in a voice off?

MS: It was in the book. The question was whether we should use it or not. If we hadn't had the *off* point of view of the woman the film would have been much shorter. It has to be there. It's a film about day-to-day life and in that life people get married. If you get married there's a wife, a girlfriend, kids, all kinds of things. The film is about that in particular – the everyday life of a family that is part of organized crime. The mother-in-law is important as well, very important because the hero talks to her. When his wife comes to him in prison, the mother-in-law is in the car. She's got to mortgage the house to pay his bail. The mother-in-law who has never had anything

24

to do with the gangsters! They're really poor people. Their entire life has been wiped out.

Goodfellas *is a film without God. And yet in the long helicopter sequence it's possible to imagine that God is watching Henry. It's the moment of judgment.*

MS: Yes, you can take it like that. God's eyes are following him; the party's over. It's a film about life. I think it's possible to detect a moral point of view in it, but I don't think I put it there. I hope that when people see the surface of the film they will have the feeling that comes from watching a certain way of life. After that it's up to them to decide whether it's good or bad. Jimmy Conway was an honest crook. He wasn't the sort to send his kids to a private school and say "My children don't know what I do." You know, he's called his children Frank and Jesse like the James brothers. [*Laughter.*] When his kids watched films on television he always told them to see whether the bad man was winning. Jesse Burke got himself killed two years ago – it was to do with drugs. He was twenty-two. The people we see in the film are not smooth talkers, they're really hard men.

Henry's betrayal is different from Judas's.

MS: It's quite simply the world he lives in. Henry Hill was always an outsider because Jimmy Burke,

Jimmy Conway and Paul Cicero were linked by a kind of code of honor; they've never denounced anyone, never given any names. Henry Hill, the outsider, allowed himself to be seduced by the prospect of making money from this kind of business and also by the life-style of gangsters. Taking and selling drugs destroyed him. When you're involved with so much money, above all when it comes from drugs, you risk heavier prison sentences if you are caught. The young members of the underworld or the mafia are so involved in drugs (because there's a lot of money to be made) that, when the police catch them, they prefer to give them names at once. They don't want to be shut up for twenty-five years. In the past you made a lot less by denouncing others. You would go to prison for two years for a minor offence and then you got a sentence that was hardly heavier for stealing ... or something else. But drug trafficking normally means you are shut away for twenty-five years and it's from that moment that people started to give others away. What happens (and Nick Pillegi made me notice it) is that now, in this underworld, crooks are less professional. In a way they've almost become dilettantes. Unlike Burke, Mario, Conway or Cicero they don't have the strength to stand up to pressure; these others had enough to stand by their principles. It's up to you to judge whether it's good or bad, I'm simply talking to you about a certain kind of society. For example, I met the policeman who arrested Jimmy Burke; he was handcuffed. They were in an airplane over JFK airport and Jimmy Burke looked out of the window before exclaiming "To say that at one time all that belonged to me." The policeman, who in fact had a certain respect for these guys, told me that afterwards he started to explain to Burke that if he agreed to cooperate his situation could be made easier, in other words the prison sentence, the reasons behind the accusation etc. Jimmy Burke didn't even let him finish and interrupted him to say "There's no point in saying that to me..." The other replied "I know, but I have to." "I know, I know," said Burke. "Let's consider the matter closed." A conversation between gentlemen. The policeman admitted to me that at the moment when he broached the subject he knew that Burke wouldn't let him finish his sentence. It was a formality and he already knew the reply. With Henry Hill it's different; in three seconds he admitted everything, because twenty-five years behind bars were waiting for him. And if he had been put inside he wouldn't even have done his full time; from outside Paul Cicero would have paid people to kill him. And for Henry Hill there was no question of rotting away for twenty-five years in prison, because he wasn't at all used to prison life.

Your film depicts the fifties, sixties and seventies. You could see it as a metaphor for the history of Hollywood. In the fifties there were rules and now everybody does what he wants.

MS: I don't say that in the film, but if you want to see that... Other people have told me that the film retells the history of the United States since the war. I suppose it's because it shows an aspect of daily life in the States that isn't so far from us. But above all we see America in the fifties. I grew up then when America was the country where everything was possible. And it's still the same today. There are still a lot of immigrants from the Soviet Union and South America. In New York it's becoming more and more difficult to find a taxi. First of all the drivers don't speak English, but that's not a problem... But as well they don't know the town! [*Laughter.*] That means that you have to try to explain to them in more or less every language where you are going. It's up to you to do the work. To be honest the question of language doesn't bother me much. But if, as well, the driver doesn't know the town, taking a taxi is becoming a real test; you have to know where you are going and make yourself understood; show him where to go [*Scorsese waves his arms about*]: "Watch out, no not there, here." [*Laughter.*] Nowadays New York is more and more like the Third World, while

Los Angeles is beginning to look like the old New York.

To return to the fifties, it was certainly a period of possibility for all of us. But in a different way. America was tomorrow's world. You had a picture of it that was like those you saw at universal exhibitions... It was a society of consumers, of plenty. From the beginning of the sixties things changed. Everything got worse and finished up with Vietnam and the kind of revolution that followed. Then there was this break, which is still going on, with the seventies. In some ways the film follows this evolution. But the character can't do anything; he's a child of the fifties and then he grows up...

I saw a documentary at Venice called Hollywood Mavericks *in which you featured. Can we think of you as a maverick, in other words as an independent?*

MS: I don't really understand the meaning of the word "maverick." Do you mean someone who manages to work within the system?

Yes...

MS: OK, but can you tell me how many good mavericks there are in Hollywood? In the end, what contribution they have made? Take the case of Orson Welles. I only met him once – thanks to Warren Beatty who was kind enough to call me one

29

evening to say "I'm lunching with Orson Welles tomorrow, come and join us." It was at the Carlisle hotel (*sic.*). We talked for a long time. He said – I think it was to Henry Jaglom to be precise – that I was a maverick. He told me that he very much liked *Raging Bull.* That was in 1982. And I recall his having used this word "maverick." The danger for a maverick is his survival within the Hollywood system. Welles couldn't survive in it. In itself that's not serious. He would only have made *Citizen Kane* [1941], or *Touch of Evil* [1958], or even *Mr. Arkadin* [1955]. Splendid, that's enough for me! [*Laughter.*] That outstrips everything, we are way beyond what we call the "classics." Godard said that Griffith taught us everything during the period of silent films and that during the talkies there was Welles. Fine, but what does a maverick do? How does he or she survive? Who were the other mavericks at Hollywood? ... Robert Rossen perhaps.

Nicholas Ray ...

MS: Yes, but, if I'm not mistaken, he was part of the system all the same; not at all in terms of the themes he tackled, but... Perhaps I'm wrong, you know. You are probably more familiar with this period than I am. On this subject here's an aside. I was American and like all Americans I used to go to the cinema. We'd see Nick Ray's films and say "That's amazing," and then go home. [*Laughter.*] Finish. We didn't know anything else, we didn't realize. You had a distance that allowed you to see differences, to notice things. We were simply in it completely. We appreciated these films, but couldn't work out how they worked. I'm talking as a viewer, and then even after I became a film enthusiast and then a student. You see, I began to study films, not the history of Hollywood. That's very different and so I wasn't able to see that. What you say about Nick Ray is interesting, but he made films for studios, first of all for RKO and after for MGM ... who else?

Columbia ...

MS: Yes, Columbia, that's perfect. He made *In a Lonely Place* [1950] for them, which is one of my favorites. After that there was Warner Bros. You see, what's interesting in his case, is that he always went from studio to studio, whereas someone like Minnelli, let's say, stayed for a long time with MGM. The luckiest ones were those who found a studio to take them in. There they could make their films and express themselves through what they made. You could consider Nick Ray a maverick because he had to go from studio to studio to express what he wanted to say – that's what I do as well. Although Universal have been very generous to me over *The Last Temptation of Christ* (they are going to produce my next film as well),[3] I have to say that Warner Bros. always saved my life, year after year, from *Mean Streets* to *After Hours* by way of *Alice Doesn't Live Here Anymore*. I adore them; they have always supported me. The people from Universal never approached me until the day Tom Pollock arrived. Mike Owitz's agency put me in contact with him and immediately after we made *The Last Temptation of Christ*. It's fascinating what the arrival of one person can bring. There I'm talking about my career as a whole. Universal were never interested in the kind of films I made. All the others – Fox, Columbia, Paramount, Warner Bros. – have always been very interested. The five major studios are always very open, everything depends on the budget, which, to my mind, is a valid reason, knowing that the films I make don't attract large numbers. I have to pay attention to the amount of money I spend therefore. To return to your question – what is a maverick?

There's also the question of style. In Ray's films the heroes were very feminized, losers.

MS: Yes, that's absolutely right. Once again you see things more clearly. I don't know. I adore Nick Ray's films, but for me he's always been a very complex figure. I couldn't talk about him the way you do, but I really like his films. My two favorites are *In a Lonely Place* and *Bigger than Life* [1956], but the directors who have influenced me are more like Orson Welles. There are the films of Minnelli as well which I like very much. I like them very seriously, but I don't think they interest us for the same reasons. I like them for formal reasons, but I also admire their vitality, their cheerfulness and their beauty… They're often in extremely bad taste, even look like picture stories, but I love that. Apart from Welles, Powell and Pressburger, Carol Reed and Hitchcock, there's one director who has had an enormous influence on me and that is Samuel Fuller. I remember seeing his films when I was quite young: *I Shot Jesse James* [1949], *Park Row* [1952]… It was as though I'd been slapped by these films; they woke me up. By that I mean that what struck me most of all was the way he simply used the camera, the lens, to tell the story. I couldn't express what I felt when I saw his films; I often see them again on television and each time I am completely overwhelmed by the way he uses music and his equipment moves … and, I have to admit, by the violence as well. His way of setting the scene immediately attracts attention. Some people find that affected, I don't. It's not only the violence, but the emotion it generates. Lots of the scenes are not really violent; it's a continuous violence, all the more terrifying because you feel that it's ready to explode at any moment.

Do you recall the completely nightmarish nature of the last montage of *Shock Corridor* [1963]? It's worse than a horror film and I find that very powerful. I also like *Forty Guns* [1957] a lot. But I do have a few reservations about his dialogs and his way of drawing certain characters. Let's say that for my taste they're not complex enough. When I watch his films it's difficult for me to say what I would have done in his place; I'd probably develop the characters more. I like to combine the two. But his way of holding the camera ... even in his new film, *Street of No Return* [1989]. In this film there is an unbelievable use of the camera and editing, and a very simple use of frames. I don't mean that the frames are simple but that his use of them is ... I've seen several scenes and when you watch you have the impression of being a kid still trying desperately to use a camera. I don't know whether the film is completely successful, I'll wait until I see it on a proper screen, but from what I've seen on video ... there's a love scene in the film; there's a mirror and the girl on the bed with the guy. The way he films this is really more interesting than a lot of things I've been able to see recently. I haven't seen a lot, but you know, you always learn something from Sam ... All the films of these people are saved. What worries me most at present is the condition of the negatives of Orson Welles' films. No one knows where the negatives of *Mr Arkadin* and

34

The Trial [1963] are. I think that *The Trial* is now in the public domain in the USA. Where is the negative? At MGM, for example, Ted Turner has all the negatives of Minnelli's films. He has all his magnificent films – but he looks after them, he restores them. It's true that he colors the black and white prints, but he doesn't color the negatives, only the backup video. We're against that, we detest it. But then again, these people, and others like Roger Mayer, have taken care of these films and have restored the negatives. On the other hand – and it's what is most odd – we're in the middle of a moral battle with them. They say "That belongs to me, I'll do what I want to it." We say "No, it's public property, it's something of the highest importance." They answer "No, it's mine, it's up to me to do what I think is best." They don't destroy the film. In my view what they do is more perverse: they destroy the way future generations will see it. Still, their negatives are restored, they are in excellent condition – no doubt in better condition than a lot of those we would like to find. As far as Orson Welles is concerned, we need to trace those who hold the rights to his films and having found them we can at least try to restore them. After that we'll have to see...

Your strength is to have created your own family of technicians and actors. Does that give you security?

MS: Yes, though not really. You can get all you want from people you work with regularly. I like working with Michael Ballhaus very much. Thelma Schoonmaker is an old friend. We like working together and we're always happy to see one another as well. Sometimes we spend hours together before starting to work. We talk about politics or films, we yell at one another and then after a certain time we say "On with the work, back to the film!" [*Laughter.*] She cuts out newspaper articles for me because she knows I never read them.

It's the kind of friendship that stimulates me. Being with people you like, learning from them, working with technicians who have been in the trade for a long time. I started the pre-production of my next film with a man called Henry Bumstead. He had been a scene designer with Paramount in the forties, fifties and sixties... He made *The Man Who Knew Too Much* [1956], *Vertigo*. It's a pleasure to listen to him. We're going to shoot in Florida, he's an adorable man. He must be approaching sixty. He loves Florida because he can play golf... I love listening to what he has to say about Hitchcock. It's the same with Freddie Francis. I hope to make my new film with him because Michael Ballhaus isn't available. I like the films he's produced a lot – those Hammer horror films. It's a real pleasure to work with people like that, but when you try to work with people like Bumstead or Freddie Francis for the first time, you don't know what will come of the collaboration. I'm always a bit nervous, because you don't know whether you're going to get on as perfectly as you'd like. You don't always know what the relationship is going to produce, but generally you can see when you meet the person. Shooting is always very trying. It's preferable to work with friends. It's always a pleasure with Ballhaus. Néstor Almendros is marvelous, very gentle. We haven't made a long footage together yet. I made this little thing, a documentary, for Armani.[4] It's a pretty little piece. It lasts half an hour. Just shots of clothes and materials, with a short interview with Giorgio. In 35 mm. I love watching Néstor working. You have the impression that it's very easy but in reality it's very complicated. But when you watch it seems easy. With Michael Ballhaus it's always very enjoyable and we've often worked together. He takes my "shot-list." I've got into the habit of doing a sketch of each shot – that goes back to the time when I worked with a small budget. You couldn't rely on the cameraman. It's preferable when you are making your first film, unless you are lucky enough to meet someone who is experienced and with whom you can communicate. But then there are two risks. First of all, you think that you could never make a film without him. You should never let that happen;

37

everybody disappears sooner or later. The second risk is that if he leaves you, you become completely vulnerable. You need to test yourself, work with people who are complete strangers. They're there to help you realize what you want, or at least to make things easier for you by bringing something. You must be able to have any kind of relationship with the one who comes first. You must be able to make the film you want to make, even if your whole team drops you. Even if it means working with different people each day you must be able to realize your film. You have to learn to rely only on yourself. During my early years I used to sketch all my shots, even close-ups, to show them to the cameraman. "Close-up, head and shoulders, OK?" [*Scorsese talks to an imaginary partner, like Tarzan to Jane – laughter*] You have to be as simple as that because some of these guys would say to themselves that I didn't know what I was doing. It was fight all the time.

[*Off*] **Robert de Niro**: *Excuse me Martin, but if you have a couple of minutes I'd like to say something to you in private...*

MS: OK. I'm sorry, I could go on talking like that for hundreds of years. [*Laughter.*] I'm coming...

Notes

1   The first record of a Punch and Judy show was made in 1662 by Samuel Pepys.
2   *The Age of Innocence* was released in 1993 starring Daniel-Day Lewis, Michelle Pfeiffer and Winona Ryder.
3   *Cape Fear* (1991) was distributed by Universal.
4   *Made in Milan* (1990).

Clint Eastwood

Unforgiven is a Western that is relatively different from the ones you have made before or in which you have performed. Why do you want to take up this style again, and how, according to you, does this last film differ from all the others?

Clint Eastwood: I can't tell you exactly why I wanted to make a Western again, there was no reason why I should or shouldn't. It wasn't a decision that was part of a precise direction I was taking, there was no prior reason in fact, and that made the project all the more exciting for me. I prefer to do things without knowing where I am going. So, why a Western? It seemed to be the only genre possible that used history, because in fact everything stems from history. In any case I've never thought of doing anything because of a fashion, on the contrary I've always felt that I should go against it. Besides, I probably feel a bit guilty always to have sought to go against what is successful and fashionable.

As for what makes this Western different from the others, it seems to me that it deals with violence and the consequences of violence more than in any of my previous films. In the past a lot of people were killed gratuitously in my films. What I liked about this story is the way violence is perpetrated and causes certain consequences. It's a problem it seemed to me important to talk about today – it assumes proportions that it didn't have in the past, even if it has always been there down then years.

Unforgiven *is dedicated to Sergio Leone and to Don Siegel. What connections does your film have with theirs?*

CE: To my mind the film doesn't have much in common with Sergio and Don. But at the same time you never know the extent to which things or people you have or have not worked with play a part in what you do, whether it's John Ford, for example, or others. These are two people I've worked with at important times in my life and, ironically, both have died during the last few years. That's why, whether they have anything to do with the film or not, I wanted to pay tribute to them, because they have had such an influence on me. I like to think they would have enjoyed the story, perhaps not – but I think Don would have liked it a lot.

Did you get involved with the script over the theme of violence, for example?

CE: The theme was already in the script as well as the repercussions it had, whether on the victims or the perpetrators. In a Western the theme is interesting because the Western is always constructed around violent behavior, the point when men become violent. And *Unforgiven* focuses on certain things, especially the theme of justice. It's possible to think the whole story would have been changed if the character of Little Bill Daggett [Gene Hackman] had done justice to the women from the start. His lack of involvement when faced with an act of violence, and even his tolerance of it, is what prompts the story – straight towards his death.

Is there a link between the political situation in the United States today and your film?

CE: You can draw comparisons I think, but that wasn't intended at the beginning. Basically it was to do with eternal preoccupations, not just those of a precise period, but given the present situation in the States it seemed to me that it was the moment to make the film. Although the script of *Unforgiven* had been in existence for a long time I was quite influenced at the time I made it by a certain number of recent events.

Like the Gulf War, for example?

CE: No, I wasn't thinking about that or about other international conflicts, but rather about those that exist at home and from which America is suffering today.

You became involved in the American political scene when you became mayor of Carmel...

CE: Yes, but I was only mayor of Carmel for two years. And during these two years I nonetheless shot two films, *Bird* and *Heartbreak Ridge*... I was a Republican since I had joined the party when I did my national service in the early fifties, and I voted for Eisenhower as president, but I rather consider myself to be a "free thinker." My political choices are not for any party and in fact I feel free, in the sense that I think that you have to leave people alone and respect individual freedom.

Do you think it would be possible to trace your personal evolution through your films, since all of them in a certain way tell a human story, namely yours?

CE: In fact I prefer to say that on the one hand there is a little of me in all my characters, and on the other that there is nothing of me in the characters I've had to play. There's no basic reason why I should be in agreement with any of the characters I play. Some in no way share my philosophy, others probably do

44

more. I've played some good "losers," like the one in *Honkytonk Man*, for example, men who destroy themselves. But I've chosen to play them because I know a lot of people like them and they fascinate me. So, though I'm not like them, basically I've seen a lot of these men who destroy themselves, who don't exploit their talents when they have some... Some of my films more than others have a message I'm in agreement with. And in the end I always see an implicit message, which reflects what I am.

Is it true that Unforgiven *will be the last of your own films in which you will appear as an actor and that from now on you will only perform for other directors?*

CE: I began to make my own films in 1970. At that time the only way I could direct them was to play in them... At the time it was a practical matter. Afterwards I got a taste for it. There was one film, the second or third in which I didn't appear [the third film, *Breezy*, with William Holden, which was a commercial failure...]. Then I'd continue work the two [things] together when I was really taken by a project. But from now on I don't think I'll do the two so much. Performing in a film is much more work than directing it, and so from now on I reckon it will be easier for me to let someone else have the job of directing when I am performing, or to perform when I am directing.

You're a producer as well...

CE: Yes. But it's easier to be a producer and an actor than an actor and director.

Is there a difference for you between films like Pink Cadillac [*Buddy Van Horn, 1989*] *and* The Rookie *on the one hand, and on the other films like* Bird, White Hunter Black Heart *and* Unforgiven, *or in your opinion are they part of the same evolution?*

CE: I think they are all different because no one of them is linked to another, it seems... There can be similarities between certain characters, in the problems they try to tackle, but I don't think there is any real connection. And if there is, I probably haven't made it regularly.

Do you consider the first to be commercial films and the others as being more difficult to get into?

CE: I don't think of the commercial aspect when I make my films. In this respect I totally agree with what John Wilson says in *White Hunter Black Heart*: "I'm not going to let eight million popcorn eaters tell me what I should do." If you are constantly thinking about public reaction you'll stop thinking about directing, because the film will then end up being organized around ready-made ideas, based on a hypothetical public expectation. It's impossible to tell a story with ideas like that. And more often than not your work gets worse with that kind of compromise. What's essential is to stick with what you want to say, with the impressions you want the film to express. Only after that is it up to the public to accept it or not. Having had both experiences, it seems to me that in the end you have to trust in fate. The public appears to know what it wants and doesn't want to see, it appears to sense whether a film is acceptable or not.

Your production business, Malpaso, has collaborated for years with Warner who distributed your last film. Are you completely independent?

CE: Yes, I'm independent. Warner have distributed most of my films and have shared in financing them, but I work in complete freedom. The people at Warner have given me a lot of support for more personal projects, like *Bird*, without there being any commercial obligation that would have distorted the film. It's not *Batman Returns* [Tim Burton, 1992]... And in the end I think they liked the film. Not all films can be big commercial successes. But you have to try or the production companies could no longer allow themselves to provide the best means. Of course, it's not always the best films that are the most successful. Sometimes you are lucky, the film strikes home and people put themselves out to see it. To use a baseball term, it's a "home run"...

You've worked with two principal cameramen, Bruce Surtees and Jack Green and you seem to attach a great deal of importance to the light in your scenes. The more you go on the more this light is becoming darker. Why?

CE: Jack Green was the cameraman for *Tightrope* [Richard Tuggle, 1986], replacing Bruce Surtees when he fell ill. His work was good and I decided to give him his chance by sticking with him. There are some of my films that I consider to be luminous – the light I asked Jack to provide for *White Hunter Black Heart*, a film that is not particularly dark, for example. *Unforgiven* is simply a "stormy" film. What you have to recognize is that it takes place at a time when people didn't have much in the way of lighting, the only artificial light was by oil lamps. And so, if we were shooting a night scene and had decided to illuminate the action a lot, people would have been in their rights to ask where the light came from.

In many ways Unforgiven *reminds me of* My Darling Clementine [1946] *by John Ford, a film in which there was already this very dark light, and what you do is not completely different from what Henry Fonda does. Have you seen this film?*

CE: Yes, and even if I am not sure that *Unforgiven* is a lot like *My Darling Clementine*, I can understand what you mean. Ford's film does indeed have a number of night scenes. Perhaps I've been inspired unconsciously by an idea like the one Ford had. I was tempted to give my film light – or rather I asked Jack Green to do it – like a black and white film. The costumes and the scenery were conceived with this particular lighting in mind, like the sort you get in black and white films.

It seems that you like to stay faithful to the people you work with, like Bruce Surtees and then Jack Green, whose names you find in the credits of most of your films, or Joel Cox, your editor since Sudden Impact. *Do you want to have a "cinema family," to be with people you have full confidence in?*

CE: It's true there are people I've worked with who seem to me to warrant confidence. It's certainly much easier when you are working to be able to communicate with him, to be able to explain to him in a few words how you see things. And that's possible with the people you refer to. I've no difficulty in making Jack Green understand how I see a scene and how it should be lit. If I were to find myself with each film with a new chief cameraman I don't know, I'd have to start from the very beginning again. It's the same with my editor Joel Cox. I can telephone him because I know that he understands very quickly and very precisely what I expect from the editing of a scene.

Your films appear to be quite distinct from what is being done in the American cinema at the moment, and to depend on you alone. Do you have the feeling that you are a "lone rider" in the film world given the way you see it?

CE: I've always felt I was somewhere else in the American cinema. [*Laughter.*] In America today everything is governed by statistics and technology and to such a degree that there is pressure on you to make a kind of film on the pretext that the public is exclusively between the ages of sixteen and twenty-one. I would especially hate to have to work in this way; it seems unbelievable that you have to make films only for people in this age bracket. With a bit of luck a sixteen-year-old will be able to enjoy my film in the same way as someone who is forty or more. Why make adults stay at home because you want to make films that aren't meant for them? I remember the last time I went to France the *Cahiers du cinéma*, I think, asked me why the United States no longer produced films except for children. And it's a question that preoccupies me: why should important subjects be treated in an infantile way. If it really is difficult to get people to leave their homes to go to the cinema, you've got to be ready to take up the challenge. If not, the kinds of films produced are more and more limited.

What do you think about Hollywood today and those people who say there is too much violence?

CE: I suppose there's room for what they call "program pictures," those films with action to attract the crowds and that reflect a certain mentality that says if there isn't some action every five minutes the film will seem boring and the audience will leave the cinema. But I prefer to think – though maybe I'm wrong – that people are more intelligent than they believe, and that you only have to tell a worthwhile story for them to want to stay sitting down, to see how a character is going to develop and how the story is going to unfold, rather than saying to themselves: "I'm going to stay here because in five seconds a car is going to smash into a wall..."

Is it important for you that you are recognized in Europe as a director?

CE: Very much so. Now, in the States, *Unforgiven* has been much appreciated and people have begun to realize that I could be a director. But it all began here a few years ago. In fact the Europeans encouraged me as a director from my first film, *Play Misty for Me*. The Americans had difficulty in convincing themselves that I could be a director because they found it hard to recognize me as an actor. They would ask themselves: "Why is he doing that? Who

51

is this upstart?" and that kind of thing. In contrast the Europeans supported me a lot at the beginning and tried to see what was valuable in what I was doing. But that's something that isn't unique to me; plenty of other directors have experienced this kind of reaction in the past, particularly here in France where there are those you call "film buffs" – I think – who are interested in films for reasons other than being distracted while eating popcorn. Now the rest of the world is coming round to this way of thinking. The fact that there are schools of film studies in universities and elsewhere means that people are beginning to consider films for their artistic merit. France has been a pioneer in the creation of the cinema techs, for example, but I believe that this influence is being felt everywhere. One of my favorite films is by William Wellman, *The Ox-Bow Incident* [1943], from the forties. I worked with him once. I had a small part in one of his films that doesn't count as one of his best [*C'est la guerre*, 1958] and I asked him quite a few questions about *The Ox-Bow Incident*, which seemed to me to be a great film.[1] He told me that at the time, the wife of one of his studio supervisors hated the film when it was first projected – she thought it was the worst piece of rubbish ever to have been financed by a studio – and that the production company had in a way got rid of it by releasing it as a class two film.

But when it came out in France, it attracted a lot of critical attention and the value of its main point was underlined – what it had to say about capital punishment, crowd violence and justice. Wellman's film deserved excellent critical notices. Then it went back to New York via France and the Americans also began to see its qualities, but it was too late, the film was at the end of its run and was scrapped. That was a load of rubbish and quite unjustified. Nowadays people see it differently and, I hope, in the States as elsewhere.

Could you explain the choice of the title Unforgiven *for which there's no equivalent in French. What's more there is already a film by John Huston with the same title.*

CE: Yes, I believe I'd understood there was no French translation for "unforgiven" and that the film had been called "ime ... impitoyable," yes that's it. Huston did indeed make a film that had the same title in the fifties, I think [*The Unforgiven*, 1960]. In fact it's a good title and it seemed to me to go with the film perfectly, and since I feel that Huston's film is not one of his best, like *The Treasure of the Sierra Madre* [1948] or other classics, it didn't seem to me to be embarrassing to use it for this one.

What do you concentrate on most of all at the moment you are going to shoot a film?

CE: I try to concentrate on the story before any-thing else, because that's where everything comes together, it's the "kernel" if you can say that. Then I try to see how images can best reflect the story, how I want the story to appear and with what emotions and sonorities. In *Unforgiven* there is this storm that becomes a kind of character, a determining element; as they draw near, the three main characters seem to bring the storm with them. Things like this aren't in the scenario; they come in later. But the basis of the drama, the questions of justice and violence, all that was already in it.

In your films the artistic expression is very often linked with destruction and self-destruction, as in Bird, Honkytonk Man *or* White Hunter Black Heart. *Is that a theme you are especially fascinated by?*

CE: *Bird* or *White Hunter Black Heart* are certainly two films that deal with this theme, as does *Honky-tonk Man* with the character who has a real talent and "kills himself" before his talent has had time to be fully expressed. I find it difficult to say why this theme fascinates me. I'm attracted to it be-cause it's something you often see in real life. Take Charlie Parker, for example: it's a real mess when someone very creative and who is gifted with new ideas destroys himself as he did. No one can fully understand how a person can have so much talent, get so much pleasure from playing, and at the same time set off his own self-destruction. That's a mystery and I've probably always been fascinated by that mystery.

A few months ago we met Jodie Foster for her first film as director, and according to her it's probably easier for an actor to be a director because it is natural for him to function emotionally and intelligently at the same time. What do you think?

CE: There are indeed quite a few precedents for actors making their own films. You can go back to William S. Hart or Charlie Chaplin, Welles and so on. Directing seems to be a natural extension of acting. When you find yourself in front of the camera it's not difficult to imagine being behind it one day. If you come from editing or writing the distance is greater because you are used to working alone and you don't have the experience of a shooting team. And then the actor probably has a better under-standing of the language of shooting and of the inherent difficulties in making a film. But at the same time I can't say there's a rule for this, it's an individual matter. An actor may have the facilities I'm talking about to make a film, but deep down it depends on each person's capabilities. There are editors or chief cameramen as well who have made marvelous directors...

What do you think about the way Little Bill Daggett (Gene Hackman) behaves in your film? Do you see him as a sort of dictator?

CE: I think he's a decent guy, at least he seems to be. He has a certain charm... I think he does things properly, like a man who is doing his job. He may have a violent past, the same as William Munny I play, but he hides it behind an appearance of being reasonable. He represents the law, therefore he's on the side of the Good... But he doesn't suffer from feelings of guilt because of his past actions as Munny does. He is utterly convinced that he's doing the right thing in having a complete control over the carrying of firearms, and he believes that the violence he has to resort to for example is a lesson that will discourage others who come to make trouble in the town. He has a sadistic streak and it's not possible to know whether it's innate or whether he has cultivated it during the course of his past activities. It's also his responsibility that is at stake. Basically he thinks of himself as a worthy being; he builds himself a house so that he can settle down and watch the sunset. He wants a quiet life, but there is no way he can stop the wheel of fate...

With Unforgiven *did you want to tell the truth about the West or is it simply make-believe?*

CE: I thinks it's a story, but one that will, in a certain way, remove the mystique of the West by introducing elements other than those of the classic Western. For example the fact that things don't happen in such a simple way, that guns don't always fire in the way they should. I don't know whether that's the truth about the West, but probably the film is close to it. Curiously there are two parallel stories going on: the one of the journalist who wants to write up the myth of the West and the other that runs through the film and contradicts it completely. What pleased me in the scenario is the way these two stories meet. In the course of history everybody changes, everybody leaves from one place and arrives in another, just as in life we are learning something every day that changes the way we see things. All the characters – or at least most of them – are given a tragic lesson, and from that tragedy each can learn something.

Do you think you have told the story of revenge?

CE: I don't know whether it's a question of revenge, even if that's there in the film because of the Morgan Freeman character, who is killed. You can see that revenge wins out, but basically no one wins anything in this story, and in fact everybody loses something, whether it's just a part of themselves … or their life. And that's what happens when people indulge in violence in order to have justice for themselves.

Note

1 *The Ox-Bow Incident* won an NBR award for Best Film in 1943, the year of its release, and was nominated for an Oscar in 1944.

Francis Ford Coppola

Francis Ford Coppola: This is for the *Cahiers*?

Yes...

FFC: Do I have to wear my *Cahiers* hat then...

No...

FFC: You'd prefer me to be me, Francis?

You're known as an auteur, so....

FFC: In any case my *Cahiers du Cinéma* frame of mind is the same as my Francis one... [*Laughter.*]

Fine. Let's talk a bit about your relationship with the Godfather *saga.*

FFC: As you know it was first of all a best seller, published twenty years ago. I was approached at a time when I wasn't very well known as a director. At the time people didn't think gangster films were particularly viable, and a lot of directors had refused it. The studios took me on because they had

liked *The Rain People* and considered that the actors
had been well directed. They also knew that I was
an American Italian. The film dealt with a delicate
subject – Italian gangsters – and to entrust it to an
American Italian seemed a good idea. That's how I
found myself with the project, and I found it very
difficult because I wasn't well enough known to
be able to impose my ideas. At first they wanted
the film to take place as of today rather than in
the 'forties. They didn't like my choice of actors
either. So negotiations were difficult but in the
end I managed to convince them. They agreed to
engage Brando and Pacino, Gordon Willis and Dean
Tavoularis for the photography and artistic direction
and Nino Rota for the music. Although at first I felt
that I had little influence on the form the project
would take, I gradually succeeded in making the
film as I wanted to. Its success was instant and that
helped my career by giving me more influence than
I had had previously. But I didn't imagine making a
second part.

*What's your opinion about gangster movies? Do you like
them?*

FFC: At the time there were others I preferred but
I liked *Scarface* [Howard Hawks, 1932] very much,
as well as the very first gangster movies. But for me
The Godfather is not really a gangster movie; at the

outset it was conceived as a film about the Borgia. What's more, when I started to do research on the New York mafia I gradually discovered a whole range of interesting personalities – Lucky Luciano, Genovese. I like this part of the work when you have to do research and discover things for yourself. I learned a great deal and began to adopt the point of view that would be developed in the film.

I've read that you had included a lot of opera music in the sound track of the first Godfather *but that you removed it at the producer's request...*

FFC: No, that's not true. Nino Rota wrote the original music and I asked him to follow the style of Cavaletti's *Cavalleria Rusticana*. That was because I had discovered this opera when I was a child. I knew that it was Sicilian opera sung in Sicilian and which portrayed the Sicilian peasants, their passions and their vendettas. I also knew that the Corleone family belonged to this tradition and so in the first two films the opera was very much on my mind and I asked Rota to quote it as he composed his music. But what you haven't been told perhaps is that Paramount simply didn't like Rota's music, but in the end I had the last word.

You have always said that the structure and form of opera have influenced you...

FFC: That's true, but you have to know that my father was a classical musician. And since I belonged to an American-Italian family I had the chance to see operas most of my contemporaries didn't see. The theater and the musical theater were my two main centers of interest and I think that had an influence on me.

Were you made to make The Godfather II?

FFC: I had no intention of so doing. I was working on an idea for a movie that I found interesting – a parallel account of the lives of a father and his son aged thirty. Since Paramount seemed to want to produce another *Godfather*, and I knew that in general sequels are not particularly well thought of and in most cases simply bad, I though I'd take the opportunity to base the scenario of a second *Godfather* on the idea I was beginning to develop.

In contrast the structure of Godfather III *recalls that of the first.*

FFC: That's deliberate. When I knew that I was going to make *The Godfather III* I thought that it would be the last part of a symphonic suite in three parts, A, B, A1 – a statement, a development and finally a statement that would repeat the first – and I hit upon this idea of a trilogy. In other words, the third movie is different from the first because in between there is the second.

How were you convinced?

FFC: There were lots of things. First of all, during the sixteen years that followed *The Godfather II*, I learned that quite a few directors and authors were working on a third chapter, but for me there was no need for a third *Godfather*.

Don't you think that was a plot devised by Paramount? A kind of blackmail?

FFC: No, a lot of scenarios were written. About twenty. Michael Cimino was interested and after him Andrei Konchalovsky. I was like a guy who, when people speak about his ex-wife, says "I couldn't care less" even though it's not true. [*Laughter.*] And all through this time I really hoped that they would give up the idea. But I was also irritated that they hadn't come to me to say I could do what I wanted. They were always bringing me scenarios that had been finished and I'd say to them *"Why are you showing me these?"* I had no particular link with Paramount. What's more you could talk of several *Godfathers* because directors were constantly changing. Some of them had even written their version of *The Godfather III*! When I was making *Apocalypse Now* I was so busy that little of this meant anything to me. But things began to change after *One from the Heart*, which was a kind of sin that I was going to have to pay for for years. After this film my career was going down and I spent most of my time trying to pay off the debts it had incurred. I also realized that my most recent films, like *Tucker, Rumble Fish* or *The Cotton Club,* were being well received and at the time I was becoming interested in a variety of different styles. All the time I had the example of Orson Welles in my head. In trying to do what he wanted Welles lost the influence he had had in Hollywood; he didn't know how to keep some support there. I tried to take a lesson from this, and despite all my efforts and all my experiments, I always tried to keep a solid base in Hollywood. And after these ten years, when I learned that Hollywood wanted to make a *Godfather III,* I said to myself that perhaps I could see this third chapter as a *Godfather II,* in other words to use a personal idea and take the opportunity that was being offered. I also wanted to be recognized by the general public again. It was clear that people didn't like my experimental films; they wanted movies like *The Godfather,* and so I said to myself "If that's what whey want, let's make one." What I needed was a strong theme. Paramount had sent to me a scenario about drug rings in Columbia that didn't have much in common with the Corleone family, so I said to Paramount "Why don't we concentrate on the story of Michael Corleone? He's the main character. Al Pacino is an extraordinary actor. Concoct a Shakespearian part for him..." A few months later the people at Paramount asked me whether I wanted to write the scenario. I said I'd try to come up with an idea. And I started to do research on the Vatican and to read around the subject a lot.

Was the Vatican scandal based on authentic facts?

FFC: It had already provided material for four books not to mention press articles... It seems that in Italy, around 1979–80, there was a huge bank and financial scandal. Two hundred million dollars disappeared and twenty people committed suicide or were assassinated. The pope also died and no one knows precisely what the cause of his death was, but he was deeply involved in this business. I said to myself that for a film of epic proportions this kind of historical background was necessary. In *The Godfather II* I had used the Cuban revolution. For *The Godfather III* I said that these things had more interest in them than drug trafficking in Columbia. I developed the story against this background, all the more so because the movie had to show the redemption of Michael Corleone. By the end of *The Godfather II* he had committed a lot of sins, had caused the deaths of a lot of people. He was a broken man. As far as I was concerned, the only way to continue to explore the history of his character was to write a movie about a man growing old, a bit like King Lear. That's how I started and the whole idea developed from there.

Isn't this desire to portray redemption also a feeling you have about your own career at Hollywood? Aren't your search for independence, and having your own studio the sins you have to pay Hollywood for?

FFC: It's true that you could see it like that. But when I use the word sin, it's in the strongest sense. I don't think that what I've done at Hollywood can be considered a sin; the cinema has to be free and independent, movies have to be different. Now I can understand how a man can find himself alone. Being a father means being alone because you have to be strong. A father has to do what is good for his family and that sometimes causes conflict. The son rebels, the wife says "I don't have to listen to you, I'm as good as you are..." So I imagine that men who bear the burden of being fathers are often extremely solitary and isolated. From that I could imagine what Michael Corleone's situation was like.

Between the two Godfathers *there was a whole wave of films in the same style. You created a genre. Were you aware of that when you were working on* The Godfather III?

FFC: It's the same with literature. I knew that when I launched a series of this kind the first movie would have all the energy because it's new – the choice of actors, the visual aspects, the parallel between the music and religion, crime and the family. I knew it would be difficult to make a third film that would be original because many of the ingredients had already been used in the first two. In *The Godfather II* the structure, which embraced two different periods, was unique. In making *The Godfather III* I was aware that if I adopted the same form it would be very difficult to rediscover the same life and energy; it was the third part. So I decided to make a very personal film – the most personal of the three – in which people would be able to see most clearly what I felt.

Attention in this film is much more focused on the family with the character of Michael's daughter a kind of witness of the whole saga. That's very evident in the scene where she is taking photographs and meeting her mother at the station.

FFC: When I wrote the scenario I always had the image of my own family in mind. That was true of the first two *Godfathers* as well. My sister Talia, for example, has the part of Connie Corleone. Whenever I had to make a choice when I was working with the scenarios of the three *Godfathers* I usually took

inspiration from something I had known personally. Now I'm older and I have a son and a daughter.
I make myself create these characters and use my
children to inspire me. At first I even thought of
giving the part of Michael's daughter to my own
because she is like her, but then I said to myself
that I needed a more experienced actress. So I chose
Winona Ryder and when, several months later, it was
clear that she was no longer available, it seemed that
after all my daughter was well suited to the part and
it was easier for me to see her in the story as a whole.
When I see her in this role I feel something that
would not have been the same had it been given to a
seductive actress whom we see romantically falling
into the arms of Andy Garcia... Because I also loved
the Romeo and Juliet side of their story a lot... The
girl is very young, it's a bit like *The Leopard* [Lucino
Visconti, 1963], with the love story between Alain
Delon and the girl who is much younger than him.
I liked the idea that they are cousins and that they
fall in love with one another – the taboo associated
with that. The story tells of what is allowed and
what isn't. For me, my daughter was an ideal choice
because she is really very young. She looks like an
Italian, she is very beautiful and yet she doesn't look
like a model. In any case these films are like "home
movies." My real sister plays in them, the music is
written by my father, and that allowed me to make

The Godfather III a really personal one. I knew that it would give the film life. It's not just a routine sequel to the other *Godfathers*.

Why did you make it in Italy?

FFC: It's true I liked this idea, but I also knew that by choosing Italy the film would have more of a European dimension and the film is really about relations between America and Europe. There are new power groups developing in Europe that rival the mafia, and then the Vatican and Sicilian background justified making it there. What's more Cinecettà is an amazing and practical studio. I could have made the film in France if I had found a similar studio.

The Godfather III *is a bit like the* Twilight of the Gods [Stewart Main, 1995]. *You always feel during the film that you are saying: "It's finished, it's over..." How did you develop this aspect of the film?*

FFC: Yes, *Götterdämmerung* ... there's something of that. According to me Michael had committed some very serious sins and, as in *The Magnificent Ambersons* [Orson Welles, 1942], I wanted to punish him, put an end to his activities so that there would be no possibility of their being continued.

In fact there is no real chance of that because his daughter kills herself. He won't have any heirs.

FFC: That's true, but don't forget Vincent Corleone, the bastard, and as a bastard he's dangerous. As for the girl's fate, I made it similar to Michael's. When he was young Michael didn't want to get mixed up with his father's milieu and become involved in his affairs, but since he loved his father he was trapped. Like Napoleon before he became emperor, Michael went too far. Napoleon treacherously had the pretender to the throne assassinated and was cursed as a result. In the same way, because he has his brother assassinated he too is cursed. He has to be punished. The spectators are witness to this horror and have sympathy for him but accept his fate because that's what it's like in tragedy. Perhaps we are forgiven… In a certain way he dies for our sins. The point of this ending was to arouse the audience's horror, but as in Oedipus something else as well. We are horrified but at the same time say to ourselves "There was never such a wicked man…" The movie becomes a kind of tragic experience that the audience can draw inspiration from…

You have made much of this aspect of the film on several occasions. The conversation between Michael and his wife in the kitchen, for example… They're together again, or nearly. Then Michael gets news of a death. He has to leave the room…

FFC: What I first wanted in this scene is that they meet again and then make love, but Diane Keaton refused... Still, I think it would have been rather good to watch them make love for the last time.

In this scene the way the door separates the two characters is a repeat of the very last scene of The Godfather.

FFC: Yes, exactly...

Michael is condemned, he can't escape his fate...

FFC: Yes, it's obvious that Michael is condemned – he's a tragic character. But what's ironic is that his tragic flaw is that he wants to be good. If he hadn't wanted to become legal again he could have escaped. He would have done business with the Vatican and made enemies. Corruption would have spread and he would have become a kind of Andreotti. It's not possible to be good in a world where power is corrupt, and that's what condemns him to his tragic fate. It's a bit like a classical tragedy.

The film shows how love and family ties can exist in a world of violence and evil. That coexistence would seem impossible.

FFC: It's true, it is impossible, but it's up to the audience to make it possible. *Tucker* and *The Godfather III* tell the same story, except that Tucker is full of hope. He always thought he could work and yet he's destroyed. Just like Tucker, Michael is aware of his tragedy, but one of them sees things positively, the other negatively. What's odd is that the audience has an important part to play in movies like this – reactions are known in advance. Even in a tragedy the audience manages to find a kind of energy, no matter how sad the things that are being recounted might be...

What is striking and very moving in the film is to see how these characters underline their feelings and their family connections: "You are my brother, my sister, etc." But this all takes place against a background of chaos. How did you do this?

FFC: In a certain way the very concept of this movie had an influence on its subject matter. For example, to have chosen to work with members of my family makes the film what it is. If my sister, daughter and father had not been involved, the movie would have been completely different. A director is not a painter. He's rather like someone organizing a big fete – he invites lots of people, chooses the food and the music and then waits to see what happens.

The style is more restrained than in your earlier films... Closer to the other Godfathers *and not at all like* Tucker *and* Rumble Fish. *The form is very different.*

74

FFC: For the *Godfather* series I always used 40 mm lenses and there are no high- or low-angle shots. There's no cheating, the camera doesn't move. It's the subject that dictates that, it's a classical, Greek style.

Why did you suddenly choose to do this after ten years of experimental filming?

FFC: Because for me the three films were really one and I didn't want to have a different style in the last one. With *Tucker* I had a different style. I like a movie to reflect its subject. As in *Tucker* – do you know this English word? A gimmick? It's a gadget, like a car... I wanted *Tucker* to reflect a car, just as in *Apocalypse Now* the movie was meant to reflect an acid trip. I always try to have movies be like their subject. In the *Godfather III*, it was a classical tragedy and I tried to film it in a pure and solemn way.

You make fun of The Leopard *by quoting the opening scene to which you add a rock number.*

FFC: You call that paying "hommage." You can always be inspired by what you read in Shakespeare or elsewhere, you can quote and use it – it's the influence of artists from the past... I read this book by Victor Hugo in which he said to young writers: *I'd say this to all those young writers who haven't been born yet: I hope when you write you will steal from us!*

Take inspiration from us, plunder our work, because that's what we've done. I believe in that a lot. The young must take inspiration from the old and as they do so they gradually shape their own personality. Clearly for other scenes – the arrival at the Villa or the curtains in the wind and so on – I borrowed from Visconti. But it works.

You also quote from the two other Godfathers *– the scene in which Joey Zasa is assassinated echoes the one in which there is the attempted murder of Vito Corleone in* The Godfather I.

FFC: Yes, and like death of Fanucci in the second... The fete is an Italian one while nowadays in New York the fetes are organized rather by the Philipinnos and Puerto Ricans.

Why did you introduce the horse?

FFC: You have to vary murder scenes a bit. In American movies today people are killed every two minutes. People have run out of ideas and I tried to find something different. I liked this image of a man committing a murder in the center of New York and then charging off on horseback.

You open the film with a fete, just like the first two. It's become almost a convention...

FFC: Well, you know, it is a *Godfather,* and in each *Godfather* there is a fete or religious ritual together with an ambitious parallel sequence that makes use of violence. In *Godfather I* it was a baptism; it's the longest scene of its kind lasting twenty-five or thirty minutes against the background of an opera. I knew it was expected of me but I wanted to do it in such a way that it would give real pleasure.

In The Godfather *a bullet smashes through the glasses of one of the characters. Here's another detail: glasses...*

FFC: [*Coppola agrees, smiling.*] I thought of something precise. If you have to assassinate someone important, how do you do it knowing that you are going to be disarmed? I thought of Kurosawa, you know, at the end of *Sanjuro* [1962] with the sword and the blood [*Coppola make a gesture*] and Pschhhh![1] In this scene blood really did spurt out but the censor made me cut it. It was thought to be too frightful and I had to take it out...

From the beginning you said how you wanted to close the story with the opera. How did you manage to have the film lead into this scene?

FFC: I was pretty free with it. I arranged the opera myself so that it was played with people in Sicilian costumes. And then there were the parallel actions: the family looking on, the girl in love with Vincent

Mancini, Connie poisoning Don Eltello. I had enough material to film it in the way I wanted. It's the sort of thing I'd done in the past. I knew what I was doing, therefore, but even so people were pretty anxious when we were filming; they wondered what the result would be.

Tell us about your plans.

FFC: The press loves to talk about plans, but I don't know why. For me, a film is like a Christmas present. I like to keep it a secret. As soon as someone talks about my plans I bring up another one to put them off the scent... You shouldn't make your plans public, it's not fair. So, what are my plans?

Dracula, with Winona Ryder, the story of a prostitute and Megalopolis.

Megalapolis, certainly...

With George Lucas?

FFC: No, George Lucas's style is very different from mine. He's a very close friend but I don't know whether he'd like the style; he'd think I was mad. [*Laughter.*] The other project, *The Girl under the Glass* is a nice little experimental one, but I was very disappointed to hear that it had been announced I would have a part in it. Because of that perhaps I won't make it. I can't stand controversy before a project has been realized It's as though I was already being advised against it because people thought it was a bad idea!

Are you thinking of reworking The Godfather *for television in chronological order?*

FFC: I'm making a version for video that is different from the previous one I didn't like much. I don't think a straight chronological sequence would work, in particular for Robert de Niro and Al Pacino, so we have gone back, kept a bit of the structure and added the third film.

What do you think about the Gulf War and about the fact that there are no pictures on our screens?

FFC: It's like H.G.Wells. We're surrounded by world-wide television. When I was a little boy we would watch television in New York and wouldn't see Los Angeles. And then suddenly you could see Los Angeles, and then all America. Now it's the whole world. The French ought to cooperate. By getting rid of SECAM there would be a standard world television. There'd be a world in which nations no longer counted, only cultures. What I'd like to make are very ambitious television movies direct from all over the world. People could choose the language they wanted. And why not have a number of centers? Part of the distribution could be handled in Britain, another in Japan. I think the CNN phenomenon is a primitive version of what could happen. It would be a kind of audio-visual world system. It's amazing to think that could be possible nowadays.

It's a project that confirms your experiments with High Definition Television.

FFC: All that I said is now seen to be true! [*Laughter.*]

But this world television would be dominated either by the Americans or by the Japanese.

FFC: No, I think it could be a kind of Utopia, not necessarily under the control of the States. It could prove to be formidable. The political scene in the States is going to change. What will happen there in seven years' time will be like what is happening at the moment in the Soviet Union. There are new leaders. People watch this. They understand. I think world politics is going to change. A world state in which there won't be any schemers. I have a positive vision of the future, but I want to be part of it as well. I prefer to be controlled by people like me. What you call the American control hides a lot of other things. I've chosen to look at the world more positively. What's happened in the film world is terrible. There is no Japanese cinema, no more national cinemas. But maybe television will carry on from there. At Zoetrope there is a lot of interest. If it happens that

I make a lot of money that's what we'll do. Do you recall my studio? That was my idea. Somewhere from which you could broadcast worldwide like CNN. With modern technology you could do that. That's my big scheme – a world television. With a studio like CNN's, but with writers and playwrights – a kind of golden age of television. People keep trying to kill me off, but they never succeed. After a while I'll become what you call an "éminence grise." And people will like me. I'll be like an elderly uncle and perhaps I'll have a real influence. For ten years now they have been trying to get rid of me, but without success. We're all getting older; perhaps we should all go further in that direction... The show is over? Yes... [*Laughter.*]

Note

1 The climatic scene of *Sanjuro* is a duel to the death between the eponymous samurai and his adversary that famously ends with a fountain of blood exploding from the chest of the defeated villain.

Brian De Palma

We've never interviewed you for the Cahiers du Cinéma. *It's time we made up for that.*

Brian De Palma: Yes. What were you up to?

Let's begin with a general question. It seems that a lot of the political and social preoccupations that were in your first films have become less important in your later ones. And yet you seem to be returning to them – in Blow Out, *for example, and in your projected* Act of Vengeance, *based on the murder of Joseph Yablonski, the reformist head of the United Mine warriors, and his family in 1969.*[1]

BDP: Yes, that's true. A lot of the movies I was making in the 1970s were fashioned, they had a kindof style. But now we are in the 1980s, I'm forty years old and I'm trying to include certain political features as I did at the end of the 1960s. But, because of economic problems, it's difficult to make political films in the States and to make them pleasant, understandable or interesting.

Was Greetings *successful?*

BDP: Yes, but a lot of political films that were successful in the 1960s would not be now. At the time the Revolution was all the rage and everyone was more or less interested by everything that was against the Establishment. But it was cheap to do and the American film industry had a huge amount of money at its disposal. Small budget movies are rarely successful in the States. Three years ago I made *Home Movies*, which cost about $300,000. Ten years ago I would have needed $25,000 to make a small budget movie. It's a hundred times more now; I don't know whether it's because of inflation or simply because the cost of films has changed. To make a film and distribute it cheaply is more or less impossible.

Do you think that videocassettes will change that?

BDP: Certainly. I hope very much so, because I can't imagine what a young director can do now. It's difficult to finance a film independently and almost impossible to release it. Who are the young directors, ten or fifteen years younger than us, who will go through a movie industry that doesn't encourage them to make experimental or revolutionary films or any other sort? In my opinion the worst thing you can say about films nowadays is that they are television films. What interest is there in releasing them through the cinemas?

Of your own films do you prefer the ones that were financially independent?

BDP: When, like me, you have had a certain success in the film world, it doesn't really matter whether you are financed by the studios or not because there aren't the same sorts of control as when you are a young director. When you have made a name these problems don't exist.

Had you reached that stage with Carrie?

BDP: Sure. I'd already made *Get to Know your Rabbit* for Warners, but I was young and I had nothing more to give.

Last night I saw One from the Heart *[Francis Ford Coppola, 1982] and I had the impression that even to tackle a small subject with a more or less non-existent story a lot of money is necessary and that this money should be visible on the screen. And perhaps that's what the American cinema is suffering from today. It has to cost a lot of money and sometimes that isn't evident.*

BDP: When you speak of somebody like Francis Coppola that's something quite different. I can see what you mean. You're talking about a kind of capitalist snowball that grows and grows, but with Francis I think it's different. I'm a bit surprised and I talk with my friends about it all the time. Important directors like Coppola, Bogdanovich or Friedkin, who were superstars at the start of the 1960s, are now making films costing a lot of money that have been commercial flops whatever their artistic merits. And yet they are so important that it's like in "The Emperor's New Clothes": they hold court, they live in grand houses always full of people; everything is filtered and watered down so that they have no negative feedback: they are geniuses, billionaires...

It's like being in government.

BDP: Precisely – to the extent that you are so well protected that you don't have to face up to what isn't working in what you are doing. I think Francis's problem is that everything he makes somehow has to be a masterpiece. In *One from the Heart* there's all this technical rubbish. And Francis is a past master when it comes to manipulating the press and the media and being seen everywhere. But I seriously think that the American system destroys creative talent. It's what has happened to these filmmakers, it's because they are so isolated that they have no way of knowing where they are at. It's interesting to note that the American film industry and the importance of directors are often linked to the big studios. The director is now God and the driving economic force, so there are no more limits, no more barriers. And the result is excess – like those unbelievable castles of mad emperors. It can happen to any one of us and it scares me because these people have talent.

And what have you done to avoid this danger?

BDP: Various things have saved me. First of all I've never had a big success – all my successes have been modest ones, and I've always had to fight for the films I've wanted to make. That's not to say that I wouldn't have had those problems if I'd had a major success. But personally I often see what's not right. I don't look for shelter. I make myself watch those of my films that have not worked to see what was wrong with them.

Do you think film criticism is useful?

BDP: Oh yes, absolutely.

Could you give an example?

BDP: It's always been said that I don't have good scenarios. For *Act of Vengeance*, the film I'm making, I decided to hire a good writer. We'd work together, I'd let him write it and we'd see what would happen. I think I've got a good scenario. Whether I can get a good film out of it is another matter.

Do you think there's a contradiction between your way of making a film and a good scenario? There's always a difference between having a good scenario that has to be illustrated and introducing more physical elements, as Hitchcock did. It's the same struggle as there was at the time of the New Wave when people said "A good scenario doesn't really matter."

87

BDP: It's the old struggle between form and content, and for all major stylists it dominates everything. Basically there are two possible directions. On the one hand, the film is original because what I believe to be its substance is its visual form. On the other, in a film like *Carrie*, I can indulge myself in the most baroque style, but then I'm obliged to remain in the world of high-school girls. That keeps my feet on the ground. I don't drift off into a Ken Russell type world where there's no real or emotional basis to hang onto and where he just has to float. I'm not against that, but the problem is that in breaking up the narration you forget the audience. I used to be a great fan of Godard, but I find it difficult to see his films again now. From the point of view of style what he's done is very good, but it's like cubism. When you break the form down you realize there's something odd about it – at least, I do. Can you really hang these paintings up in your house and live with them? Or do you say to yourself "It's a fabulous, amazing idea, but now I'd like something that's a bit closer to me." From an intellectual point of view what he does is very powerful, it's a bit like Eisenstein. Some of his films were marvelous, but I never watch Eisenstein movies at home. I prefer Howard Hawks. There's always seems to be a struggle between genius and stylistic innovation on the one hand and the essential ingredients of storytelling on film on the other.

By the way, Godard is one of your fans. He told us two years ago that the only recent American film he had seen recently was The Fury.

BDP: Yes, I know. I read that somewhere. I've always admired Godard a lot. I was absolutely bowled over by *Weekend* [1967]. But when his films are being shown I don't make any effort to go and see them.

Maybe that's because a lot of what he invented or created has been copied and become commonplace.

BDP: Exactly. D.W. Griffith is another example like Eisenstein and Welles. When you study film you go to see their work and are surprised. But their films are not the sort you would have at home. *Citizen Kane* [Orson Welles, 1941] isn't shown all the time.

You can fast-forward others and study scenes that you particularly like, but from a purely emotional point of view I don't find this to be as effective as *The Searchers* [John Ford, 1956].

Don't you think that during his English period and for part of his American one, Hitchcock had a kind of golden age when it was possible to work on style without losing the primitive and popular aspects of his films? One of the reasons why the Cahiers *are increasingly interested in your work is because you've kept some of that without copying or plagiarizing Hitchcock, you've tried to keep the same quality of being simple and basic in your style and in what you produce. This seems to be just about unique in the American cinema today.*

BDP: Yes, but at the same time Hitchcock was a consummate businessman. He'd exploited television before people realized its potential importance and he made a lot of money. As far as I'm concerned the key to the American film industry is its capitalist side. We can admire what the French, the Italians or the Germans are doing, but it's not us, and I think that when we try to copy them it's disastrous. Over here we make cars, sewing machines and mixers, and we work and sell on a grand scale. It's like that and I don't think we should change.

But like Hitchcock you've got this very pessimistic philosophy that goes with this idea – this English idea that there is something sinful about business.

BDP: Basically I think that, in spite of everything that has been written about Hitchcock, when he sat down and thought about the film he was going to make, he said to himself "Will it really be interesting? Will it scare them? Am I going to get them?" It's as if he was saying "Are they going to buy this Ford?" That's basically how he thought of his films. Critics and university people can say what they like about the Catholic symbolism in his films. What really motivated him was "How can I make ten

million dollars with one million?" In my view, that's
the American system. As far as style is concerned,
Hitchcock never lost sight of the ultimate object of
the film. I put all my craziest ideas about style into
Carrie, but I never forgot that it was about a girl
who absolutely hated her fellow pupils and killed
everybody. That was what drove the film. I think the
problem for the independent director is that he says
to himself "Shit! Shit the studios! Shit the public!
I'm an artist and what I want is to enjoy myself."
Maybe he can do that, but perhaps no one will want
to see his film – and in the American system it's very
difficult to get over that because we live in a world
where you have to succeed. People read *Variety*, not
the *Cahiers du cinéma*. That's the world we live in.
How many people are interested in what's happening in the back of beyond? Everyone says "Pauline
Kael gave me a good review, and I couldn't care less
what the population in some God-forsaken place
is doing," but it's not quite true. I think what really
matters is the number of people you want to attract.

Why do you live in New York rather than in California?

BDP: The problem with California is that you're
right in the middle of this industry and you don't
have the necessary distance from it. I think economic imperatives dictate to a certain extent what
you want to do but they shouldn't dominate. In

Hollywood they are too prominent. You are always being examined and judged to see where you are at, how much your last film made, what your next one is going to be. And it has an effect. You start to say to yourself "Perhaps I ought to make Barbara Streisand's next movie."

When I saw Reds *[Warren Beatty, 1981] recently I felt that audiences are increasingly taken in by American films less and less. They don't manipulate them or trap them any more. That, for me, is style – games. And the more this happens the more I feel the cinema is losing something vital. But this refusal to play the game – which comes from Godard or Straub – is already something. But* Reds *is neither one nor the other. It's like the pages of a book being turned.*

BDP: That's just another example of the effect of capitalism on the artist; he becomes his own bank. We don't have artistic sensitivity on the one hand and commercial sensitivity on the other any more, we have the two at once. That's why there are so many directors who've run out of steam at the age of forty, like Bogdanovich and Billy Friedkin. What's happened? They've made a few good movies and now they make these odd films that have no interest, not even an aesthetic one. It's sad. I often think about that.

92

Do you feel isolated?

BDP: Not really. I'm still trying to hit the jackpot. I still want to have the kind of huge success we we've been talking about.

Apart from Cassavetes and a few others like you, there are very few filmmakers who succeed in showing the pleasure they have in making films.

BDP: I think in some ways you can see in John and me the absolute happiness there is in trying to find the money to make a movie!

And what's more, you often show people who are in film or who are interested in technique like the kid in Dressed to Kill *or Travolta in* Blow Out. *It's like a mirror that reflects the pleasure of working at technique in film – like sound, for example.*

BDP: Yes, were only too happy to be filmmakers. We don't have the feeling that it's a heavy burden to communicate with humanity. I don't have the feeling I'm writing *The New Testament* each time.

Don't you have projects that you dream about but you've never been able to realize?

BDP: Yes, of course. *Act of Vengeance* for example, the film about the murder of the Yablonski family. I've been trying to make that for seven years. Most of my projects take three or four years. For me, it's never easy. Perhaps that's what's saved me.

What has an experiment like Home Movies *meant to you?*

BDP: That was always a disappointment. I tried to teach in a college how to make small budget films like I did fifteen years ago. We made a film and had a lot of difficulty in finding a distributor; it didn't go well and it was never widely shown. It's always the same story. The students probably learned more from the fact that it wasn't a commercial success than they would have done if it had been hugely successful.

You made it at Sarah Lawrence College where you made your first film, and it seems that there are lots of things that are like those in your earlier films.

BDP: Yes. They have a lot in common. Except that the first film was made in 1963–4 and the second in 1978–9. What's dreadful is that exactly the same thing happened – it was a commercial flop – but it was a valuable experience. What surprised me was that I made the movie for $300,000 and nobody in the film world bothered about it. My reputation wasn't much use, apart from getting a few extra meetings. And I can say that it was ten times worse than before. Ten times! I had the idea when I went

94

into universities with different films. I would ask the students who the directors were of the films they were going to see, and they looked at me wide-eyed – they didn't know a single one. So I said to myself, who are these people? Maybe they need a course on small budget films. After that a few of my students went on to make small budget films and that's good. But it made me realize how difficult it is – worse than I had imagined.

Among those of your films that have not been successful are there any you prefer?

BDP: *Hi, Mom,* for example. At first it was shown at Loew's State in New York, the worst place you could find for this film, because the distributor thought it was one of those anti-establishment films, which was not the case at all. It was a very strange film. *Phantom of the Paradise* was billed as a rock opera extravaganza and it made no impression on the rock world, or the horror film world – in fact on no-one.

In Paris it enjoys a kind of cult.

BDP: Yes, I know. And my biggest disappointment is *Blow Out.* It was brought out in the middle of summer as an adventure and action movie. It was shown at a bad time and in a thousand cinemas. It's an unusual political film, full of meaning and very carefully constructed, but it didn't do well. I was stupefied when critics said it was a bad suspense and horror movie. Nobody understood it. Audiences didn't like either the character played by Travolta or the film. In the United States the distribution costs were eight million dollars or so, which is disastrous for a film that cost so much. I avoided developing the love story in this film because I didn't think the character would be interested in it. But that's what the public expects it seems when you have John Travolta and a pretty girl. If I'd made more of the fact that he falls in love with her and by mistake puts her in danger maybe the film would have been more successful. I hesitated a great deal but thought that that wouldn't interest him. He was only interested in what obsessed him and his problem was that he always relied on his skill to solve his difficulties. That's more or less how I see people. With the trio of John Travolta, Nancy Allen and Brian De Palma that film cost eighteen million dollars, but if I'd made it for five million and with unknown actors it would have been better. The various bits of the film didn't match my ideas, at least from an economic point of view. I could have realized my idea for four million. I didn't need all that show and fuss. It's a typical example of capitalist excess. I can make a big action and adventure film, but it's not right for this story. It wasn't made for that. It's rather an intellectual reflection on the Watergate climate.

Let me ask you a question about Obsession, *which is the film of yours that I prefer. I've heard it said that Paul Schrader felt a bit betrayed by the changes you made to his scenario. Is it possible to say that he felt just as betrayed by the work of Bernard Herrmann? According to what I've read this film can be considered a three-way collaboration between you, Herrmann and Schrader.*

BDP: When I'm preparing a film I put everything on cards and I build up sequences like that. When I did it for *Obsession* there was a whole third part that didn't work. It only repeated what had happened in the past by projecting it into the future and it was no longer in what Paul Schrader called the cut version that finally appeared. And when I laid the film out I said "We'll never manage this third part, the public won't understand." I'd already thought that. When Benny read the scenario he said "That'll never work," which only confirmed what I felt. And my suggestions didn't please Schrader. He said it was only the ending that gave the film any value and if we took it out we would have a kind of television melodrama. It was a big mistake and I was pathetic. And then I read that he had said that I had ruined his big project. In my opinion *Obsession* works, and *Taxi Driver* [Martin Scorsese, 1976] works. None of Schrader's films work because when he is left to himself he can't sort out his structural problems. It's when you have directors like Martin Scorsese or me who know how to get something worthwhile out of these stories that they are successful. I've been rather bored by this business, but I hope his flops will make him realize that he is not the structural and formal genius that he thinks he is. It's another example of a director's megalomania. I remember, when he showed Martin and me a tape of *Hardcore* [Paul Schrader, 1979] we suggested a lot of changes, and the film came out more or less as it was on tape. There was a period in our lives, or perhaps because we were poorer, when we listened to what was said to us. We appreciated constructive criticism. Unfortunately that's no longer the case today. The only ones who are still open to this way of working are George Lucas and Steven Spielberg. It's unbelievable what Steven and I passed on to George for *Star Wars*!

Do you show your films to Lucas and Spielberg?

BDP: The last time I did was with *Home Movies*. But the problem is that we live in very different places. That's what success is: you run all over the world. Lucas and I are planning to make a film together with Spielberg, and that would be good. This collaboration between directors is something I miss, and Steven is one of the few who are open to it. Me too. We all started like this in the early 1970s, but we don't do it any more. It's a shame.

After Phantom of the Paradise, *which I like a lot, are you tempted to make another musical comedy?*

BDP: I've thought about it. I like that, but nobody has really made a successful rock film. Rock-and-roll had a powerful influence and there must be a way of using it in a movie. It's one of my ideas.

What do you know about your public?

BDP: You have the public of your successes. Movies that work create a public for that kind of film. When I make films like *Carrie, The Fury* or *Dressed to Kill* a certain number of people come to see them. But when I make something different like *Home Movies* or *Blow Out* they are a bit disappointed. If I had to make *Blow Out* again I think I would do it differently, because I think I have lost some of my audience. It's the same for *Phantom*... I thought that *Dressed to Kill* would be demolished by the critics because of its similarity with *Psycho* [Alfred Hitchcock, 1960], but, on the contrary, I received one of the best lot of reviews of my career. I was really surprised.

Note

1   *Act of Vengeance* was eventually made for TV by John Mackenzie (1986).

Joel and Ethan Coen

Where did the idea of Barton Fink *come from? Did you work on the scenario together?*

Ethan Coen: Yes, we had been thinking about it for a long time. It came to us in the middle of writing *Miller's Crossing*. The work on *Miller's Crossing* was going very slowly and we wanted to take a break and write about something else. It took us very little time – three weeks. At first we wanted to create a part for John Turturro and we were also thinking of writing something for John Goodman.

So the idea began with two actors and your wish to see them in the same film together?

E: Yes, we'd already worked with them – Turturro in *Miller's Crossing*, Goodman in *Raising Arizona* – and we were seduced by the idea of seeing them in the same film. What interested us as well was to give them parts and a situation that would be different from the ones it had been possible to see them in before. The story developed from that idea. Barton, a writer, was the starting point and motivator of the story.

Is he inspired by a novel?

Joel Cohen: No, he's invented. What was important for us was the background he came from. We thought about writers like Clifford Odets, but Odets was very different from Barton and his Hollywood experience had nothing in common.[1] He came from New York and the Broadway theater and went to Hollywood to write for films. So there were two common points between them.

E: We didn't set out to make Barton like any real or even fictitious character. He's a bit of everything. Your guess would be as good as mine if you set out to try and discover what inspired us when we created him. It's strange for us to have created a hero of a film who is so unattractive. [*Laughter.*] Who knows what perverse impulse made us do that.

J: The film does its best to abuse Barton. It attacks him. We tried to create a character who deserved the fate that we wanted to keep in store for him. [*Laughter.*]

E: We wanted to have a character who was vulnerable and full of illusions… in such a way that at the end he would have to forget them.

102

J: The most sympathetic character in the film is probably the one played by John Goodman.

Except at the end.

E: He's consistent. He's found an odd way of dealing with his problems. [*Laughter.*] He's a character pursued by his own demons and in a way you can't help feeling sorry for him. He's more aware of all this than Barton is.

That's what saves Barton Fink: at the end Karl spares him because he has been self-centered enough not to be afraid of him. Barton's biggest fault is his self-centeredness and it's because of that that Karl allows him to live.

E: That's true enough. His ignorance helps him a lot…

It's like Kafka… in fact, the film made us think about Kafka a lot.

E: But I don't know whether there is really a reason for sparing Barton. Talk about Kafka if you like, but I think as far as Karl is concerned it's like a whim… Let's say that on that day he was in a good mood. [*Laughter.*]

You don't want to talk about Kafka?

E: I don't read Kafka. This morning even at a press conference someone referred to Kafka and said there were similarities between our film and *The Castle*, but to tell the truth, I've not read any of his novels.

J: I must have read some of his short stuff.

E: But the parallel is rather good for us, so there's not a problem... [*General laughter.*]

It's another of our ideas as critics... We thought there were other parts that weren't literary in origin: you talk about Hollywood and the studio could be Universal's

J: The only bit of reality that inspired us was Jack Warner. He had had himself called "General" and had ordered a uniform from the studio's costume department. But that's one of the few authentic episodes we were inspired by.

E: And ironically it's one of the most surreal details in the film...

How do you get on with your studio?

J: We have an excellent relationship with the studio that distributes our films in the States. Our films are financed by small companies based in Washington, but, since *Raising Arizona* it's 20th Century Fox that distributes them. It works well. So you shouldn't see in *Barton Fink* any possible hint of problems we might have had with our studio. [*Laughter.*]

104

What is most striking about Barton Fink *is, once again, the way you approach a genre: you have the material for a screwball comedy [the sophisticated comedies of the 1930s]. In simple terms it's the story of a disturbed writer in Hollywood. And as in the gangster film* Miller's Crossing *or the thriller* Blood Simple, *you change and twist the material in such a way that the ending we might expect is not what happpens ... Is this a conscious way of working on your part? To start with a genre on order to write against it ...*

E: No, not always. If we talk about how we started, with *Miller's Crossing* and *Blood Simple*, we wanted to tackle a precise genre: the gangster film, with *Miller's Crossing*, and the *film noir*, with *Blood Simple*. With *Raising Arizona* we obviously didn't think in the same way. But you don't necessarily think about a particular type of film when you start to work, and that's certainly the case with *Barton Fink*. You're right to say that the material at the outset could have been that of a farce. But we didn't try to tie the film to a particular genre.

J: There are other films that have points in common with ours. Do you see what I mean? If you take the characters who are alone in the world ... the writer in the hotel ... People have talked to us about *Shining* [Stanley Kubrick, 1980] ...

E: To come back to this idea of genre, when you've worked on one, as with *Miller's Crossing* and *Blood Simple*, the public expects certain things, certain typical situations that it was amusing for us to change, to subvert...

Do you enjoy playing with conventions?

E: Yes...

Even within a single scene: you begin it letting people think that it will end in a certain way and then the opposite happens.

E: With *Barton Fink* we wanted the spectator to feel destabilized, like the character of Barton. He's lost in an environment that is strange, almost hostile, and we wanted him to lose himself in it very slowly, just like the spectator, without knowing what is going to happen.

How did you manage to convince a studio to help you produce a film whose subject is a guy all alone in a bedroom? [Laughter.]

E: We were very surprised as well. [*Laughter.*]

Did a turning come in your career with the critical success of Miller's Crossing?

E: Although *Barton Fink* is distributed in the States by 20th Century Fox it was financed by this small company, Washington Circle Films, that produced it even before the conditions for its distribution had been finalized. We didn't have to discuss matters with the studio in making the film.

J: The film was produced therefore outside the studio system, even though it's a studio that distributes it...

E: The decision had already been taken before the release (which wasn't very good) of *Miller's Crossing*, but the critical success of the film nonetheless helped us.

In Barton Fink *as in* Miller's Crossing *you manage to give a dynamic direction to the film simply by using a single character who spends his time motionless, standing, sitting or lying down... The very form of the film contrasts with the character's passivity.*

E: For *Barton Fink* we really had to ask ourselves how, in an interesting way, we were going to film that – two characters in discussion, Barton in front of his typewriter, alone in his bedroom. This is very different from other kinds of scenes which, in a certain way, provide their own reply. It was difficult to know how to film sequences that were less dynamic.

But when you come to writing, how do you go about it? Do you note, for example "Barton writes," and then on screen the same scene is like an Orson Welles' sequence shot.

J: What really happens is that at the moment of writing our visual ideas, the position of the camera, the layout of the shot are already foreseen. In some cases it's very detailed, in others not at all. It's all a bit arbitrary. For example, there's the scene where Barton is thinking, the camera goes in all directions, settles on the sheet of paper in the typewriter and then suddenly we see him and the secretary in the waiting room of the offices. All of that is detailed in the scenario. But in contrast other moments have only been finalized later.

But you always run the risk of filming a scene in a way that is not appropriate... You're aware of that. I mean what is most astonishing in the way you go about things is that it works, it doesn't appear to be gratuitous... How do you do it?!

J: Our problem was as follows: how to make something static move, how to add a bit of drama, of emotion that might attract the public...

E: It doesn't always work but you can't see that in the film, because those are the bits we have cut out. [*Laughter.*] We tried lots of tricks and some of them didn't work. Don't let on. [*Laughter.*]

You can rely on us. Tell us about the significance of the Bible in the film...

J: It's really a simple joke...

E: Any excuse is good for a bit of a laugh. [*The Coen brothers laugh.*] We were writing and it's as simple as this: we asked ourselves what we might find in a hotel bedroom in the United States. In every hotel bedroom in the States there is a Gideon's Bible...

But your choice had been made.

E: Of our text?

Yes.

J: It was our chance to take ourselves for God. It's the author's privilege. [*Laughter.*]

Why does John Goodman shout "Heil Hitler" before killing the policeman?

E: You might think it's a bit of a gag, but it's a sort of break intended to show that this guy is really unhinged.

In terms of movement and rhythm the ending of Barton Fink *is very different from the one in* Miller's Crossing *where everything is explained and comes together at the end – without any climax, but it's fascinating to watch. In* Barton Fink *you have the opposite; it's hard to think that at the end the film reaches such intensity of madness and destruction. Did you play on this kind of fake restraint at the beginning of the film in order to push the public in a particular direction?*

E: In a gangster film the public prefers to see things in their place, to develop and then conclude, it's like that in *Miller's Crossing*. In *Barton Fink* we didn't want to make a film that went on it's ordinary way, that's the reason why the ending is not as neat as that.

J: What is being talked about doesn't take place at the very end of the film – the fire, the kind of madness that explodes like that. The real end of the film takes place on the beach. It's true that there are two powerful moments in the film: the one when he wakes up and discovers the girl's corpse, and the one when he enters into a different kind of reality with the fire in the corridor. Everything is different from the logic that has come before. We did that deliberately – starting the film so that the discovery of the corpse is a completely unexpected surprise. In fact that's the sort of thing you can't do within the rigid structure of a specific kind of film and what's more it upsets the balance of the film. The kind of shift that takes place at the end of the film with the fire is deliberately intended to create a different reality. Even if it is not done in too disturbing a way it's nonetheless in keeping with the rest of the film.

E: But the question is an interesting one. How much freedom are you allowed to have to change the nature of the film and surprise the public's expectations? In this case we had more freedom than in *Miller's Crossing* or *Blood Simple*.

What's common to both Miller's Crossing *and* Barton Fink *is that they are like nightmares.*

J: *Miller's Crossing* has nightmarish parts, but *Barton Fink* really is a nightmare.

E: For *Miller's Crossing* we conceived a scene with the set designer and the cameraman, and in our discussions with them we clearly stated our intention of giving a nightmarish quality to one scene – the one in which Johnny Caspar guns down his associate in his office by shooting him in the head. But that wasn't our intention for the film as a whole.

J: *Barton Fink*, though, was really conceived as a nightmare from start to finish with its dreamlike atmosphere. Take the last scene of the film on the beach. That emerges from an intangible logic, the logic of dreams rather than an intellectual logic. This scene is appropriate for the film as a whole: it's the closing image and brings something to a resolution.

E: It's interesting that if we talk about films in this way it's because of the freedom that we're allowed.

111

The story can be manipulated, the idea of a dream can be turned into a nightmare.

It's a film about initiation and perhaps sexual initiation.

J: Yes, that's interesting. In fact, I think John Turturro sees the story in the same way. We haven't discussed it in that way, but the comment seems to me to be right. At the end the character no longer has the same certainties; he's been educated by the character of John Goodman.

At the beginning he's a virgin.

J: We had talked to John about that; he's like a small boy leaving his house for the first time. He's all alone. Even the music we asked Carter to write [Carter Burwell composes music for the Coens' films] has a kind of innocent, childish melody. And his relationship with Audrey as well...

She's a mother figure...

J: Yes, up to a point. It's interesting to see it like that.

Is the other writer Barton meets based on Faulkner?

E: You may think of Faulkner when you see him, but it's like Barton and Odets; Faulkner is only a starting point for the character, no more. There's only a superficial likeness – a physical one with that part of him that was the southern writer with a drink problem.

Fitzgerald as well...

E: Yes, but Fitzgerald was a Yankee... Faulkner was a man from the south, a Southerner.

J: He was also an alcoholic, but that didn't stop him writing, unlike the character in the film.

In Blood Simple *you alternate interior shots with exterior ones – the bar, the motorway, the houses. In* Raising Arizona *everything is outside. And in the last two films practically everything is shot inside, but you avoid creating an historical dimension and tend to go towards something abstract; there are no or few details indicating a period...*

E: Your comment is interesting; we really wanted to avoid an historical recreation.

J: The other reason is the limited budget imposed on us. If we wanted to shoot outside, like Sergio Leone, we'd have needed twenty to thirty million dollars.

E: That's why the outside scenes in *Miller's Crossing* take place in woodland...

J: Because a 1929 forest is exactly like a 1990 one. [*Laughter.*]

E: But it's true that these two films are filmed indoors punctuated by outside scenes: The forest in *Miller's Crossing*, the beach in *Barton Fink*...

Are you aware of the spectacular change in tone and style between your first two films, Blood Simple *and* Raising Arizona, *and the last two?*

E: At the moment when we realize them and write them our films have a considerable importance for us, but to be honest with you, when they are finished we don't really think about them and try not to compare them.

J: Once a film has been finished we don't look back at it. We don't see them again. It's too painful [*laughter*], we only notice our mistakes.

E: We thought about *Miller's Crossing* for a year and a half, and now it's finished. [*Laughter.*]

Are you close to other filmmakers in Hollywood?

E: Sam Raimi is a really close friend. But in our normal daily life we see very few filmmakers.

J: We live in New York and most people in the business are in Los Angeles.

Have you seen Darkman *[Sam Raimi, 1990]?*

E and J: Yes, and we liked it very much.

114

Do you see any common features between your films and Sam Raimi's?

J: We do things very differently. We don't like the same things. But we admire his technique and his style a lot. And he's someone who helped us a lot when we were starting...

Don't you have the feeling that in your last films, you are doing something that Hollywood didn't expect from you three or four years ago, at the time of Blood Simple *and most of all* Raising Arizona?

E: Yes. They're probably really fed up with us. [*Laughter.*]

What we feel is that Hollywood was counting on you, was waiting a while before you took over from the wonder boys like Spielberg...

E: Probably, yes... but we hadn't made any promises. [*Fresh bursts of laughter from Ethan and Joel.*]

After your first two films you achieved a certain artistic power in Hollywood. But what has come since has nothing to do with that... People almost have the impression that you have taken advantage of that in order to do things that are completely the opposite.

E: You're getting onto a delicate subject there.

J: We write what we want and if someone agrees to finance them we'd be mad to refuse. But it's true that we have had some surprises, as with *Barton Fink*, for example. What makes us different from other directors is the way we work. When we've finished writing a scenario we always remain close to it. There are no big surprises. That's why our scenarios are so detailed. If we talk about audiences, we believe that a film that doesn't attract the public is a failure.

When we knew that you were going to make a gangster film, at the time you were starting to work on Miller's Crossing, *we expected to see another brilliant achievement, a spectacular film, full of scores being settled...*

E: Yes, and it's pretty conventional...

No, restrained, controlled rather... The dynamic of the film is elsewhere, in the relationships between the characters and in the way it is constructed...

J: It's the old question of style. People always separate style from the rest – the subject or the characters. What's important is the most appropriate way of dealing with a situation or a scene. In the case of *Raising Arizona* the style matches perfectly what we wanted to say, but it seemed more obvious, more visible. When you have a guy on a motorbike who spends his time shooting rabbits [*laughter*], you can allow yourself all kinds of original and strange camera angles, and give the film an energy that's a bit insane. In *Miller's Crossing* you have the story of a depressed Irish gangster who stays at home asking himself how he is going to get the better of his enemies. That other style wouldn't have been right... It's not the best way of portraying a depressed Irishman. [*Laughter*.]

OK, but that didn't stop you in Barton Fink *from having the camera spin round in the bedroom...*

J: Yes, but that works in a different way. The internal logic of the film is different. The subject is not a normal one... The intention is almost surrealist. It's subjective, it's to do with what happens to him and how he sees these things. The film shows how the character is assaulted by outside forces to the point where it all becomes a bit unreal. And here again the style of the film reflects that, and so you can have the camera spinning and going down the drain in the washbasin without its being in any way shocking...

All the more so because it's his brain, his head that are going in all directions...

J: Exactly, it's what you were saying just now about the dreamlike quality of the film. And as with a dream these are things that you can accept.

117

The dreamlike side of *Miller's Crossing* works in a different way and doesn't allow ... in any case I don't really see that film as a dream.

What projects do you have?

E: We haven't begun to think about them yet, but we're going to start...

J: Soon...

Note

1 The playwright and screenwriter Clifford Odets (1906–63) was a champion of the poor and underprivileged who, although a member of the American Communist Party, survived investigation by Joseph McCarthy and the House Un-American Activities Committee in 1953 and continued to work in Hollywood.

Tim Burton

You left Disney's studios a few years ago. Why are you going back today?

Tim Burton: I went back because of *The Nightmare Before Christmas*, basically because Disney held the rights! When I had the idea ten years ago I was under contract to them. In fact, I'm not completely sure whether they really do, since I was working in an environment that was very odd. I was constantly "giving birth" to ideas and I don't know whether that one belonged to them. At the time I was also making other things outside, more personal things... But they seemed to have the rights and that's why I had to come back to them. They've given a lot of support to this project. They've become very successful with animated films and they understood it. That's the good side of things. The bad one is that the project cut across a lot of their usual productions. When you work with Disney you have to take two things into consideration: the studio itself and its public reputation. Inevitably that caused problems since I didn't feel at ease on either side. Disney's public reputation can become very onerous, especially when you are trying to work. Even so, Disney supported the project and enabled it to exist, and that's very positive.

Would you say that The Nightmare Before Christmas *represents the dark face of Disney?*

TB: I remember the first time I worked in the Disney studios. It was all so smart I was overwhelmed. But perhaps Disney has always had this dark side. It would probably disappear under a good layer of sentimentality, but it was there. In some of their films you can feel it coming through. Today it's perhaps even more noticeable.

How did you have the idea for this film?

TB: I frequently begin working on something with material that's quite old. I think that when you've grown up in drab suburbs with working-class people and petty, white, puritan members of the bourgeoisie, you are hungry for rituals, for color, for all these basic things. These people have no real sense of culture, of belonging anywhere, nor do they have the capacity to express themselves to those around them or even to members of their own family. That's what explains my taste for the films Corman made based on the stories of E. A. Poe, for anything that seemed to me to have a bit of life to it. I think that *The Nightmare Before Christmas* originated from my taste for the festive seasons, from a wish to recreate this kind of feeling. Doctor Seuss's books were with me in my childhood. At that time the telly showed a festival of cartoons called *Rudolf the Red-Nosed Reindeer*. I always loved this kind of cartoon, just as I loved *How the Grinch Stole Christmas* [film from a book created, written and illustrated by Dr Seuss]. All those festivals, and especially Christmas and Halloween (with masks as night fell and so on), have a special feel to them. Perhaps you don't have the equivalent of Halloween in Europe. These festivals bring with them a whole series of images, with particular rituals linked to particular places. I think I began to think about this film after the short film *Vincent* when I was already interested in this kind of animation. It was a bit as if I was writing a poem. There's a famous American poem entitled *The Night Before Christmas* by Clement Clarke Moore. I've given my own reading of it in the voice of Doctor Seuss that I've called *Nightmare before Christmas*. At first I wanted to make it with Vincent Price. It was to have been a short, and I had even thought of giving him the role of narrator. But that was ten years ago and things didn't work out like that. The project was under wraps with Disney all that time.

Is there a difference between the technique you used ten years ago and the one you use now? Is the animation completely computerized?

TB: Absolutely not! It's unbelievable but the technique has barely changed. The only difference between *Vincent* and *Nightmare* is that a computer controls the camera's movements. Everything else is exactly the same as it was a hundred years ago. It's pixelation... Another difference is that I worked with a team from San Francisco – really gifted artists! It's wonderful to see them draw everything instead of pushing buttons. Of course computers can produce surprising things, but an artist's hand has something that is so fine and so solid! I believe manual work expresses an infra-verbal, unconscious energy. It has nothing to do with what can be done on a computer. And so the technique has hardly changed. Most of the optical effects, the use of mirrors and so on, all that has existed for a very long time. I've simply had the opportunity to work with a team of outstanding artists.

What part did the drawer Henry Selick have in making the film and what was yours?

TB: We needed three years to make this film. [*Laughter.*] It's like a film in slow motion! Given the way we went about it I didn't have to be there every day. Fortunately, because I would never have

124

been able to do everything I have in the meantime. Maybe we filmed three shots each week and that produces only a very small amount of the negative. And that was all! But it allowed me to go and see the images and make a number of criticisms. Henry Selick draws magnificently. He was responsible for most of the pixelation. I had worked with him at Disney. We produced foxes, dogs and so on. After that he went to San Francisco where he worked a lot for MTV but still carried on with a lot of personal research. Excellent things. At the time, San Francisco was the home of a group of good animators. Henry really became responsible for the technical aspect of this project. He knew most of the group and he was there every day to supervise them. He really put himself into this project and did some excellent work. For me it was ideal because I could go and see the work in its finished state. Animation is extremely painstaking work and you have to keep the right distance from it, so I had the luxury of being able to look on from a distance and to be there to see what worked and what didn't. That suited me perfectly because I was working on *Batman Returns* and on *Ed Wood*, and every time I went to see how they were getting on it renewed my energy.

The most interesting feature of The Nightmare Before Christmas *is the way that, as the film goes on, the animated characters become more and more human, especially the hero, Jack.*

TB: That's something I've always tried to do. In some films you are aware of the puppet, in others their movements are so perfect and it appears so real it gives you gooseflesh. I've always tried to deal with my characters as though they were real people. Quite often in animation people keep their characters as puppets, but try, nonetheless, to have the audience feel that they are real. Of course, for animators, who spend two good years with these characters, they are real. They become attached to them. That's what pleased me most of all when I was working with the group. A good animator is like a good actor, it's simply that the process is very much slower.

Do you see a continuation from your first short films – Vincent, for example – and Edward Scissorhands *or* The Nightmare Before Christmas? *As a viewer I can see one.*

TB: I think there is an inner logic that is always followed. On the one hand there is the theme of the quest: Jack is looking for something positive. And on the other, there is the theme of perception: This character can be seen to be frightening, but is he really? For me the film is built around one central theme: a character who is basically good is looking for something positive, but which others see as negative. In fact it's the classic story we've had since Frankenstein – the way we perceive people and things. It's a theme you can find in the films of Ed Wood as well as in those of Vincent Price. My personal contribution has been to take this issue further, and it probably permeates everything I have done. When the film came out audiences felt a bit unsettled because they knew that Disney was involved. They found there were bits that were terrifying, too horrible. Children loved it, but parents, adults, found it too horrible. And that was the precise subject of the film. In the event reality really became part of the fiction. The result was strange.

Although they are apparently intended for children, in reality do your films perhaps mean something to adults?

TB: I remember going to a showing of *Pinocchio* [Hamilton Luske, Ben Sharpsteen, 1940] a few years ago. When the whale appeared on the screen all the kids were scared, but even more so were the parents – to the point where they took their children out. That film made a big impression on me when I was small. These are decisive experiences in life. If you don't allow children to see the slightest negative image how are you going to prepare them for life?

Especially if you don't let them see these things in imaginative works! After all, this sort of thing existed well before the cinema and television in fairy stories and even in prehistoric cave drawings. I've always felt very strongly that all that prepares children to face life in a more gentle way. And the imagination can be very healthy since it is based on certain psychological realities. I don't think I have ever produced anything that is negative. I'm always very impressed by films that show violence in too credible a way; even if it is treated satirically violence is too close to reality. It's like that that the barriers between reality and fiction are upset, but as long as you confine yourself to the imagination it can't be harmful, it seems to me. My strongest childhood memories probably come from Corman's films, in which violence certainly played a major part, but they didn't make me particularly violent. On the contrary, they helped me become aware of things that were deeply repressed. What's more, in the United States, when you study the personalities of serial killers, guilty of so many dreadful actions, you find that for the most part they've grown up in a very repressive environment, sometimes even a very religious one that was intended to protect them from all bad influences. Everyone has his dark side and everyone has to repress things, but the best you can do is probably to let them come to the surface. And in order to do that there's nothing healthier than to watch fantastic films. There's no better outlet.

Do you believe that the cinema has a cathartic role to play?

TB: Exactly. Society is constantly changing. I think that films that depict problems to people nowadays, like *Theater of Blood* [Douglas Hickox, 1973], for example, are pretty gruesome. If I were a kid today I don't think I could stomach them in the cinema. And yet I only watched that sort of thing at the time. No doubt I've got my bad side today, but I'm not the sort of person to do someone in by chopping them up.

Are you interested in psychoanalysis?

TB: Up to a certain point. It can help me analyze how I react, to understand human nature. But I'm more interested in perception. I grew up feeling that others were judging me. I strongly believe that everyone is judged, pigeon-holed by society. That seems to me to be quite harmful. It's why I was so receptive to all those horror films. In *Frankenstein* [James Whale, 1931], *Creature from the Black Lagoon* [Jack Arnold, 1954] or *King Kong* [Merian C. Cooper, Ernest B. Schoedsack, 1933], the creatures are perceived as monsters, but those hunting them never are. And so, taken as a whole, the way in which society perceives individuals very often doesn't take account of certain things. That's frightening. It's something I've tried to struggle against all my life. It's as harmful as racism that is only one part of it. No one can escape, everybody is catalogued, and color makes no difference, in a way that is more or less violent, more or less definite.

Is a director like you a kind of Doctor Frankenstein?

TB: Certainly. Making a film is always a bit like making a witches' brew. It's true that when you are working you have the same passion, the same madness, as the Doctor Frankenstein of the first film. And when you make a film you never know how it will turn out. That's what's so good about it in fact. You have an idea of what you want to do, you work like a madman and it's great. You mix up all sorts of strange things without quite knowing what that will produce at the end of the day.

You appear to enjoy very considerable freedom. You've made an animated film, a documentary and a film about a director who, to say no more, is atypical (Ed Wood). How do you explain this freedom that is surprising in the present context of American productions?

TB: *Ed Wood* is probably the smallest budget I've worked with since *Pee-wee's Big Adventure*, and it's also the one that was most difficult to realize. Personally, since I've been directing, I've never gone into a film saying that it was atypical. I simply made the film I wanted to make. I never thought in terms of the kinds of films that were popular in Hollywood, or in terms of what was considered to be normal. But with *Ed Wood* I tried to explain to the producers who refused to chance themselves in this venture that I was doing it at union rates without looking for any other profit. In terms of investment the risk was therefore limited. But the film was long and difficult to produce because the studios didn't really want to produce it. At first I was supposed to do it with Columbia. The problem at Hollywood is how things are perceived. I've often wanted to ask "But if you're expert, why don't all the things you produce make a huge amount of money?" Producers are so arrogant! I'm not claiming that my judgment is infallible, but how can they be so certain?

Wouldn't it be better to work with independent producers for this kind of project?

TB: I don't know. I've always had special ties with Hollywood. I had the chance to make the films I wanted to make. I've never made an independent movie, I've always worked with studios. As a result I've always felt myself to be in a strange position. I know people who have worked with independent

producers. Each system has its advantages and dis-
advantages. After all, a producer is there essentially
to find money. It's of little importance whether the
work is taken on by a studio, by a rich individual or
by a bond company [a term describing a financial
organization providing insurance to cover possible
budget excesses], by a generous German producer
or by Warner. It's you who has to answer to the
producer for the way in which the money has
been spent. In all cases of this kind you can expect
problems. As someone who has basically worked
with studios I can see the positive and negative
sides of the experience. In fact I don't know the independent cinema well, but then people I know
in that system have had the same problems even
if the financing has been different. But I'm open to
everything and perhaps one day I'll give it a try. I've
always accepted films that I make in my way, and
up to now I've been lucky because the public has
gone along with them. But when you've got a certain
following it becomes very difficult to negotiate. With
Ed Wood I constantly had to remind those who were
questioning me that I was making the film at union
rates and that it was a small budget film. And even
when it was a matter of finding a set, people would
say to me "Ah, you're the person who made *Batman*,
you must be a multi-millionaire!" I must have given
up a lot of things because of that. People always

wanted to squeeze money out of me. Because five years ago *Batman* was hugely successful people tended to see me as a kind of Hollywood nabob. I had the same experience with *Edward Scissorhands*. The outside scenes were filmed in Florida and I very much wanted to shoot one scene in a swamp. They wanted to build a set on a tiny piece of unused land infested with mosquitoes. And simply because I had just made *Batman* they asked a ridiculous price. They wouldn't have dared try that with anyone else. I had to give that land up, like a lot of other things. I almost felt penalized by my own success. I almost wondered whether I wasn't going to take a pseudonym so that I could realize my projects on a small budget. No doubt that would have allowed me to work as I wanted. It's an oddly heavy label to have to carry around.

You were saying that it took a very long time to make Nightmare, *but it's clear that you needed a lot of time for* Ed Wood *as well.*

TB: Yes, I take my time and it's very enjoyable. With films like *Batman* the date of their release is fixed before the scenario has been finished even. What's more, you don't have a definite scenario while the people at McDonalds are pestering you to know what this or that character is going to be like, because they're in the process of making products based on them. It's really crazy when you're making films of this scope! To make a film like *Ed Wood* that is on such a small scale that no one really believes in it allows me to take my time.

Why did you choose to shoot this film in black and white?

TB: As far as I am concerned the debate between black and white and color has always been badly put in Hollywood. What matters is to know whether the way you do it will be right for the film's atmosphere, in the same way as the artistic direction, the scenery design and everything else that contributes to it. Unfortunately Hollywood puts a brake on everything. Nonetheless there shouldn't be such a fuss about black and white. As it happened, in no way was I claiming to make a film with artistic pretensions. It simply seemed to me that black and white would be better. Once again it's a matter of how things are perceived. What's important is to know whether people will take to the film or not. And it seemed to me that it would be better in black and white. And there are a number of reasons for that. Among others, how could I film Bela Lugosi in color when I had only seen him in black and white? The characters he has played have become real figures. And the Bela Lugosi I was showing was already very old, at the end of his career, already faded so to say. In any case I wanted to do justice to Ed Wood, to his films and to recreate the atmosphere of the time... I've always felt uncomfortable with those films in color that claim to recreate the golden age of Hollywood. I don't find them believable – maybe because Hollywood is already an artificial place. There are three points to remember: these films are based on real people, they are situated in Hollywood and recreate a certain period. Among all such films made recently in color I don't know a single one that has pleased me, however well made it may be. Ed Wood was such a strange guy and his followers were all so odd, even in real life. I tried therefore to put them into their own context, to be as realistic as possible. Quite simply I couldn't manage to think of them in color. It's an emotional thing.

Ed Wood is practically unknown in France. Is he well known in the United States?

TB: In the States Ed Wood has become something of a cult. When he died in 1968 his death was not even reported in the papers. You can't say he was famous therefore. But he had made a certain number of films... I saw *Plan 9 from Outer Space* [1959] on television when I was a kid. The film made a strong impression on me, mainly because certain parts seemed to indicate that the action took place at Burbank, near to the cemetery and airport, just near to where I lived. I had the impression that all these things were happening there in my neighborhood. The film had such a strange character that it was as though it was true. The surrealist style, the writing and the characters made it very real for me. That's how I first perceived Ed Wood. Then, around 1980, I read several books whose authors classed Ed Wood as the worst director of all time. At that moment there was a feeling that he was a sort of cult figure, with films like *Glen or Glenda* [1953] and others. Of their kind his films are unique. I've been to screenings where people have fallen about. The films are really unbelievable. You can laugh at them, but personally I have always found a certain depth in them. But what is talent? That's the real question. After all there are plenty of bad films, but to be the worst director of all time you must have something special. All the same, Ed Wood had a strange talent. It's often very difficult to distinguish the success talent brings from what determines failure. Quite often people have been very divided over my own films. I remember when *Pee-wee's Big Adventure* came out in the United States it was ranked among the ten worst productions of the year. The dividing line between the worst and the best is sometimes very hard to draw. Rejections often teach you more about the people who make them than about the films.

136

Two or three years ago a biography of Ed Wood came out in the United States. Were you inspired by it?

TB: It's an interesting book. It's not really a biography though, rather a collection of interviews or parts of interviews with people who worked with him at the time. Normally I can't stand biographies, but what interested me was that these people had very different views. When I watch filmed versions of biographies I often find them very flat, lifeless. That doesn't interest me a lot. In contrast, what made this book so interesting was that it became clear that people couldn't rely on their memories. It has to be said about this lot that they drank a great deal! They appeared to be completely adrift. Straightaway their memories didn't match and it seems that because of that we're nearer to the truth – in any case, to the truth of memory that tends to embellish the past. In fact, since the book appeared, these people don't tell their story in the same way. They are constantly revising their recollections. And I find that much more realistic. I'm no different; like them I tend to embellish the past. After I've finished a film and go home, I promise myself to do everything to avoid undergoing such a trial again. But after a year or two, I make another film and I gradually have an excellent memory of this dreadful experience. That's how memory works. That's what makes this book so interesting for me. It allowed a great deal of freedom once there was no obligation to retell a life about which there would be so much information. I would never have had the nerve to take my inspiration from a book that was a real documentary. I would never have dared transpose that onto the screen with all the faithfulness that was required. With this film I tried instead to evoke what touched me about Ed Wood, to show how I perceived what was particular about his films. Ed Wood was curiously optimistic ... but in a perverse way. I read some of his letters. He had his dark side, but he was incurably optimistic. When I'm shooting I sometimes think I'm in the process of making a masterpiece and people don't realize it. I think he pursued this delusion to an extreme.

It was Martin Landau who took the part of Bela Lugosi.

TB: Yes! What a superb actor! Brilliant! At the end of his life Bela Lugosi had become someone very strange, just like the characters he played. He took so many drugs that he had become emaciated. It would have been difficult to recognize the Bela Lugosi who had played Dracula. He had a kind of nobility that was quite decadent. And Martin Landau managed to get into the skin of this character. He had to be made up, obviously. I rarely find makeup believable, especially when you're dealing with a real person, but on this occasion the work was magnificent. We created a new character. It was unbelievable to see.

What is the principle behind your documentary on Vincent Price? Are interviews included?

TB: The film doesn't claim to be a documentary about Vincent Price's life. That has already been treated. I've seen several films of this kind. What interested me was to have discussions with him. I didn't want to have a chronological approach embracing all his life. I simply wanted to talk about certain things and show certain extracts. I wanted to talk to him about the impact he had had on me. When all is said and done, this film puts the last pictures we have of him together and is the echo of certain conversations I was able to have with him. In this way I had the chance to give some representative extracts and identify his personality, his mind, rather than give an account of the circumstances of his life. At the end of one's life one doesn't see things in a strictly chronological way, but in a more subjective one. This film gave me the opportunity to have a conversation with a man who had achieved great things during his life.

Where did this admiration for Vincent Price come from?

TB: I think that with horror films, in any case for those he made, many viewers feel the need to have sympathy for or to be in contact with someone they admire. As far as I was concerned when I went to see his films (and especially the series based on the work of Poe) I almost felt as though I was undergoing analysis. These films helped me to understand, to feel better. I felt at one with them because I had been very alone when I had grown up, very enclosed, and life around me seemed to be very abstract. These films often deal with this kind of feeling. Vincent Price took on so many challenges, so many sufferings ... he played people who were sensitive to anything strange to life – to death, to all those abstract things, to horror. He (or at least the characters drawn from the work of Poe) seemed to see quite clearly all these intangible things, whose importance I could sense myself. I used to go and see his films like going to an analyst.

Which of Vincent Price's films do you prefer?

TB: Probably those made by Roger Corman: *The Fall of the House of Usher* [1960], *Pit and the Pendulum* [1961], *The Tomb of Ligeia* [1965]. But in fact I love all of them. I like his first films, those by William Castle and even his more recent English films like *Theater of Blood*. They were really good. But the ones by Corman are probably the ones I prefer.

You like small budget films, as is shown by the fact that you have devoted one to Ed Wood, the king of the small budget film. You like Corman's films. Do you think that films made today are too expensive? Not yours particularly but those produced by the film industry in general.

TB: That's a difficult phenomenon to analyze. On the one hand, films effectively are expensive, but on the other, once on the screen, the investment is poorly estimated, just as poorly as the use of a credit card is. But there is another side to this: these films provide work for a lot of people, and that's very positive. What's more, going to the cinema is still quite cheap compared to other forms on entertainment. I know that, personally, when I go to the theater in New York, for example, and spend fifty dollars on a ticket, I'm slightly uneasy at the idea that perhaps I'm not going to like the play and then the evening will have cost me a lot. I'm not particularly bothered about the cost of films. Naturally, when you do the sums the cinema is expensive ... And the more expensive the film, the more I feel pressure from the outside. Anyway, I prefer to keep to a reasonable budget so that I don't have that pressure.

Is Ed Wood *a small budget film?*

TB: According to Hollywood's criteria, yes. I think the average budget keeps increasing. At present, a film costing twenty-five million dollars is considered reasonable. And a film that has cost forty isn't thought to be an exception. When I made *Batman*, a few years ago, it was considered expensive, but today films easily cost forty million dollars, even if it's sometimes difficult to see where the money has gone. It's a bit vague. But the higher the budget, the stricter the control exercised by the studios. You always have to compromise. Even so I think I've come out of it rather well.

The press recently made a lot of the contract you were to have signed a few months ago with Michael Ovitz. Is it true and what are its terms?

TB: I signed this contract two years ago. I changed agents for several reasons, but more than anything because I wanted to become involved in a new relationship.

The idea of having an amusement park based on the world of your films is no longer on then?

TB: I don't like what happened. I find that pretty unpleasant. Basically I'm only interested in the cinema or the stage... I've nothing against writing once that gives me the same feeling as when I'm shooting. In the same way I try to make films that are likely to make the same impression as those I enjoyed when I was a kid. But in fact I could do anything as long as I can experience this feeling. Maybe I could even paint the statues on Mount Rushmore! The moment

I can do what gives me pleasure where the backing comes from doesn't matter. I've never wanted to be part of those Hollywood deals, and I see no reason to start now. I find that sinister. I don't want to have anything to do with it. I detest seeing America, and indeed the whole world, being invaded by these amusement parks. It scares me. I would far sooner stroll about in an old-style amusement park with its ghost train, big dipper and everything...

If you were approached to make video games, do you think you would agree?

TB: I'd only accept on the understanding there were certain implicit conditions. I'd never accept a proposal that was too vague. Once again, as with a film, I must be able to do what I want, to convey that feeling or impression that I'm looking for something. I've always wanted to go to Las Vegas, not because I gamble particularly, but when I went as a child I found the atmosphere of the place surrealist. All the old images of Las Vegas appealed to me. I'd love to put on a crazy opera there, even a show in the Las Vegas tradition. But I don't like what the town has become. And so, given the way our culture is developing, I wouldn't throw myself into a project for such a thing that was too vague. I'd like to create something that is more moving, as I have tried to do in the cinema.

Is Batman *really over and done with?*

TB: Yes, I think so. It seems to me that for the studios it's big business. They've got all those toys to sell, rights to exploit. And as far as the last one is concerned I don't want to get any more out of it. They want to do their thing, which is to exploit the rights. I don't think they look at it in any other way. I can understand that and accept it. I'm going to find myself in a strange situation. I can make all my views and opinions about it known to them if they really want me to. I'm obviously still attached to the subject because it's a world that means a lot to me. It's a bit like having brought up a child and seeing him take off on his own. I'm still very close to *Batman,* and I'm ready to advise in all kinds of ways if the studios want me to. But I have to cut myself off a bit since *Batman* belongs to them.

Who are your favorite directors? Do you like Fellini, for example?

TB: Yes, of course. I haven't seen all his films. I've a lot of respect for people who have original personalities. I respect them even if I haven't seen all their films, the same with David Cronenberg. And yet, I haven't seen *Naked Lunch* [1991] nor *M. Butterfly* [1993]. I have respect for Roman Polanski who's made lots of things I like. I have respect for people who follow their own line, whatever it might be.

Isn't that the problem for a director like you: to follow a personal line in spite of the pressure that comes from a big industry?

TB: Every time I watch a film, in Hollywood or elsewhere, I'm upset a bit. Each day reminds you that you are working for an industry. And even if you go to see a film and pay for your seat you realize you're caught up in the Hollywood machine. As far as I'm concerned I prefer to keep clear of all outside influences. If you go and see a film that is doing well and you find useless, you can't help asking yourself questions: Why is it so successful? Why do people flock to see such and such a film and not another one? I don't want to clog my mind up with questions like that. It's clogged up enough already!

Filmographies

Martin Scorsese

The Departed	forthcoming
No Direction Home: Bob Dylan	2005
The Aviator	2004
Gangs of New York	2002
Bringing Out the Dead	1999
My Voyage to Italy	1999
Kundun	1997
Casino	1995
The Age of Innocence	1993
Amazing Stories: Book Four	1992
Cape Fear	1991
Goodfellas	1990
Made in Milan	1990
New York Stories: Life Lessons	1989
The Last Temptation of Christ	1988
The Color of Money	1986
After Hours	1985
The King of Comedy	1983
Raging Bull	1980

The Last Waltz	1978
American Boy: A Profile of: Steven Prince	1978
New York, New York	1977
Taxi Driver	1976
Alice Doesn't Live Here Anymore	1974
Italianamerican	1974
Mean Streets	1973
Boxcar Bertha	1972
Street Scenes	1970
Who's that Knocking at My Door	1967

Clint Eastwood

Million Dollar Baby	2004
Mystic River	2003
Blood Work	2002
Space Cowboys	2000
True Crime	1999
Midnight in the Garden of Good and Evil	1997
Absolute Power	1997
The Bridges of Madison County	1995
A Perfect World	1993
Unforgiven	1992
The Rookie	1990
White Hunter, Black Heart	1990
Bird	1988
Heartbreak Ridge	1986
Pale Rider	1985
Vanessa in the Garden	1985
Sudden Impact	1983

Honkytonk Man	1982
Firefox	1982
Bronco Billy	1980
The Gauntlet	1977
The Outlaw Josey Wales	1976
The Eiger Sanction	1975
High Plains Drifter	1973
Breezy	1973
Play Misty for Me	1971
The Beguiled: The Storyteller	1971

Francis Ford Coppola

Youth Without Youth	forthcoming
Supernova	2000
The Rainmaker	1997
Jack	1996
Bram Stoker's Dracula	1992
The Godfather: Part III	1990
New York Stories: Life Without Zoe	1989
Tucker: The Man and his Dream	1988
Gardens of Stone	1987
Peggy Sue Got Married	1986
Captain EO	1986
The Cotton Club	1984
Rumble Fish	1983
The Outsiders	1983
One from the Heart	1982
Apocalypse Now	1979
The Godfather: Part II	1974

The Conversation	1974
The Godfather	1972
The Rain People	1969
Finian's Rainbow	1968
You're a Big Boy Now	1966
Dementia 13	1963
Tonight for Sure	1962
The Playgirls and the Bellboy	1962
Battle Beyond the Sun	1960

Brian De Palma

The Black Dahlia	forthcoming
Femme Fatale	2002
Mission to Mars	2000
Snake Eyes	1998
Mission: Impossible	1996
Carlito's Way	1993
Raising Cain	1992
The Bonfire of the Vanities	1990
Casualties of War	1989
The Untouchables	1987
Wise Guys	1986
Body Double	1984
Scarface	1983
Blow Out	1981
Dressed to Kill	1980
Home Movies	1979
The Fury	1978
Obsession	1976

Carrie	1976
Phantom of the Paradise	1974
Sisters	1973
Get To Know Your Rabbit	1972
Hi, Mom!	1970
Dionysus	1970
The Wedding Party	1969
Greetings	1968
Murder à la Mod	1968
The Responsive Eye	1966
Show Me a Strong Town and I'll Show You	
* a Strong Bank*	1966
Bridge That Gap	1965
Jennifer	1964
Woton's Wake	1962
660124: The Story of an IBM Card	1961
Icarus	1960

Joel and Ethan Coen

Paris, je t'aime (Joel Coen)	forthcoming
The Ladykillers	2004
Intolerable Cruelty	2003
The Man Who Wasn't There	2001
O Brother, Where Art Thou?	2000
The Big Lebowski (Joel Coen)	1998
Fargo	1996
The Hudsucker Proxy	1994
Barton Fink	1991
Miller's Crossing	1990

Raising Arizona	1987
Blood Simple	1984

Tim Burton

Charlie and the Chocolate Factory	2005
Corpse Bride	2005
Big Fish	2003
Planet of the Apes	2001
The World of Stainboy	2000
Sleepy Hollow	1999
Mars Attacks!	1996
Ed Wood	1994
The Nightmare Before Christmas	1993
Batman Returns	1992
Edward Scissorhands	1990
Batman	1989
Beetle Juice	1988
Peewee's Big Adventure	1985
Frankenweenie	1984
Luau	1982
Vincent	1982
Stalk of the Celery Monster	1979
The Island of Doctor Agor	1971

Note

The filmographies represent only directorial work for the cinema and do not include credits for work in any other category or medium.

Acknowledgments

These interviews were selected from *15 ans de cinéma américain, Cahiers du Cinéma*, 1995. Translated here by John Flower with permission of *Cahiers du Cinéma*, the selected interviews were initially conducted as follows:

Scorsese, Paris, 1990: Interview by Patrice Rollet, Nicolas Saada and Serge Toubiana, September 11, 1990, translated from the English by Nicolas Saada. Published in *Cahiers du Cinéma, No. 436*, October 1990.

Eastwood, Paris, 1992: Interview by Thierry Jousse and Camille Nevers, translated from the American by Camille Nevers. Published in *Cahiers du Cinéma, No. 460*, October 1992.

Coppola, Paris, 1991: Interview by Iannis Katsahnias and Nicolas Saada, February 25, 1991, translated from the American by Nicolas Saada. Published in *Cahiers du Cinéma, No. 442*, April 1991.

153

De Palma, New York, 1982: Interview by Serge Daney and Jonathan Rosenbaum, February 12, 1982, translated from the English by Odile Finkielsztajn. Published in *Cahiers du Cinéma, No. 334–5*, April 1982.

Coen, Cannes, 1991: Interview by Thierry Jousse and Nicolas Saada, May 18, 1991, translated from the English by Nicolas Saada. Published in *Cahiers du Cinéma, No. 448*, October 1991.

Burton, Los Angeles, 1994: Interview by Thierry Jousse, translated from the American by Sylvie Durastanti and Jean Pêcheux. Published in *Cahiers du Cinéma, no. 486*, December 1994.

The Introduction, The Challenge to Hollywood, is an edited version of the original by Nicolas Saada, published under the title "Les contrebandiers de Hollywood."